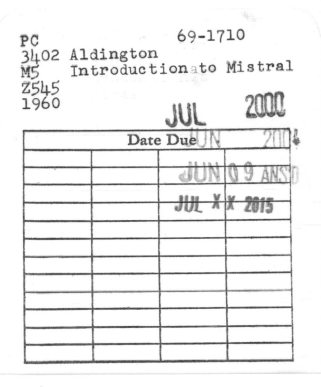

PC   69-1710
3402 Aldington
M5   Introduction to Mistral
Z545
1960

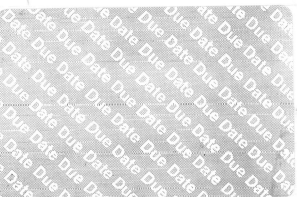

INTRODUCTION TO
MISTRAL

INTRODUCTION TO
Mistral

by

RICHARD ALDINGTON

With a Preface by Harry T. Moore

"Nous avons fait route avec les pauvres.
Il faut rester avec eux." MISTRAL

SOUTHERN ILLINOIS UNIVERSITY PRESS

Carbondale, 1960

PREFACE

By Harry T. Moore

Some writers take pen names as a wishful coloration, identifying themselves with a place or an experience. Thus the pseudonym of Jacques Anatole François Thibaud, who wrote as Anatole France, gave him a special connection with the country he loved; and thus Samuel Langhorne Clemens, his heart forever on the Mississippi, made himself known to the world in pilot's idiom as Mark Twain. But other writers have no need for *noms de plume*. One, deeply concerned with humanism, could properly write his studies of man as Thomas Mann; and Mistral was born with a strikingly appropriate name for a writer of Provence, for that is the name of the wind that comes into his country from the north on cloudless days of hard cold sunshine. Mistral's verse reflects this among much else that is quite different, but it might be safely said that his work is as characteristic of the Midi as the wind whose name he bears.

Richard Aldington's book on him is particularly welcome here and now, for Mistral, who shared the Nobel Prize in 1904, is undeservedly little known in America today. Because he wrote in *langue d'oc*—which, as Mr. Aldington points out, Mistral treated as a language and not just a *patois*—he is for the most part read over here by advanced specialists in Romance studies. Yet in his variant of what once was Latin, or in the translation of this *langue d'oc* into French or English, Frédéric Mistral has a charm, a flavor, that should not be missed by readers of various persuasions. An educated peasant, Mistral is one of the great "regionalist" writers of the world, bringing alive the wheatlands of Southern France, its gleaming coasts, its villages with their traditions dating from pagan times, its wild white horses of the Camargue on the delta of the Rhône, and the river itself, particularly the vigorous and now displaced life of the bargemen, an aspect of Mistral's work which Mr. Aldington rightly compares to Twain's *Life on the Mississippi*.

To add that the dates of Mistral's biography are 1830 and 1914, two famous years in the history of France, is enough to place this poet for the general reader before he turns to Richard Aldington's text. But a few words about Mr. Aldington will not be out of place now, for although he is one of the best-known writers of the modern world, his long association with France—which ultimately produced this book—may be discussed here with full appropriateness.

Richard Aldington first went to Paris in the spring of 1912, when he was a young poet who had shortly before left the University of London without taking his degree. In that same golden May of 1912, his future friend D. H. Lawrence also crossed to the Continent for the first time, eloping to Germany with the fabulous Frieda whom he was later to marry. In Paris, Richard Aldington saw his own future wife, the American poet H. D., whom he had known in London. Another American poet and London friend was also there—Ezra Pound, already studying and writing about Provence.

By the time of the 1914 war, when all of them were back in London, they had become the leading Imagists—"that Pickwickian word," Mr. Aldington calls it—and Pound had already broken away from the group. Richard Aldington became literary editor of the *Egoist,* in which he published contemporary French as well as British and American poets, but in 1916 he went back to France (and Belgium) in a quite different capacity, as a member of the British Expeditionary Force. His experiences in the army, first as a private soldier and then as an officer, are reflected in his bitterly satirical war novel, *Death of a Hero* (1929).

The war left him with a severe case of what in those days was called shell shock. For eight years he lived quietly in the English countryside, at first in a cottage that he took over from D. H. Lawrence, to whom he several times compares Mistral in the present book. At last a handsome payment from Crosby Gaige, for the anthology *Fifty Romance Lyric Poems,* enabled Richard

Aldington to move back to the Continent permanently. He then felt well enough to begin writing novels, and *Death of a Hero* was the first of them. Some of these books, *Rejected Guest* (1939) is one, are set in France or contain French scenes.

During those postwar years in England, Mr. Aldington had kept in close touch with French culture. He was the reviewer of French books for the *Times Literary Supplement* (London), and he translated frequently from that language. He was also putting into English the works of Greek, Latin, and Italian writers (and, with John Cournos, was translating the Russian author whose pen name was Sologub), but he was concerned mostly with French authors. Among others, he translated Cyrano de Bergerac (*Voyages to the Moon and the Sun*) and Voltaire (*Candide* and *Letters of Voltaire to Frederick the Great*), as well as the more recent work of Julien Benda (*The Great Betrayal*, Aldington's original title for *La Trahison des Clercs*) and a massive two-volume anthology of Remy de Gourmont. He even dipped into fifteenth-century French for his translation of *The Fifteen Joys of Marriage* and into fifteenth-century Liégeois for his version of *The Mystery of the Nativity*.

All of these were done before the second world war. Mr. Aldington's career as a biographer began in 1943, with *Wellington,* and continued chiefly with portraits of Englishmen such as Charles Waterford and D. H. Lawrence and T. E. Lawrence. When in the 1950's he turned to Mistral, he was richly experienced as poet, novelist, critic, biographer, editor, and translator—and he was ripe to produce a fine critical biography of Mistral in English. Mr. Aldington, who now lives in Berry, amid the low hills of the eastern Loire, was living in Provence when he wrote this book. He was seeing what Mistral saw, and he was hearing and speaking the language of Mistral.

The book itself has been a fine latter-day success for Richard Aldington. In England, its first British edition (Heinemann) was sold out; in France it was awarded the Prix Gratitude Mistralienne for 1959 by the Jury for the Frédéric Mistral Prize. Mr. Aldington in his "Author's Note" speaks of this biography as "a very informal book in which I have tried to present unfamiliar matter readably." This is true, for the reader will note the ease and verve of the style, the personal comments which are often so piquant, and the smooth translations from the *langue d'oc*. But Mr. Aldington's claims are too modest: I will end this discussion by quoting from the poet Cyril Upton, long the Riviera correspondent of the *Times* (London) and a member of the Académie of Aix: "Mistral was, as this book so rightly states, a very important man apart from being a great regional poet. His intuitive realization that an age he was actually living in was destined to fade so rapidly and that it could be kept vibrant emotionally in song, intellectually and academically in the *Trésor,* and visibly in a Museon Arlaten, is brought out with striking perception in this book. He was an example of a concentrated apotheosis, as it were, of that vague diffusion of Greco-Latin colonial expression which survived Saracen and monastic Christian interruption to become the culture of the Languedoc. I have read many studies of Mistral, but this Introduction is, in my opinion, by far the most intelligent approach that has been accomplished."

And now it is time for Richard Aldington to take over on the subject of Frédéric Mistral, his times, and his places, in a book written partly because so many of today's visitors to the Midi "innocently" ask, "Who was Mistral?"

Southern Illinois University
November 26, 1959

CONTENTS

AUTHOR'S NOTE

I wish to thank M. Frédéric Mistral *neveu, Capoulié* of the Félibres and Maître Pierre Julian, *Majoural*, for permission to quote and to translate from the poetry and prose of Mistral; also the publishers Lemerre for confirming this permission in the case of citations from *Lis Oulivado;* and lastly Messrs. Faber and Faber Ltd. and Roy Campbell for permission to quote the poem 'Horses of the Camargue'.

The best introduction to the Félibres in general (as distinct from Mistral in particular) is Mc. Julian's ?-vol. collection of their poems with detailed and accurate *notices*. Unluckily at the moment of writing it is temporarily out of print.

Since the books used in this brief introduction are mentioned in the text, a bibliography seems superfluous, especially since it would be very long. There is an immense Mistral literature in Provençal and in French, most of which I have not read, and which I have naturally passed over in silence. Similarly I have made no attempt to discuss any of the philological problems involved. Until Mistral's very numerous letters are collected, arranged, annotated, and printed, a biography is hardly possible; so I have not attempted that either.

In the interval between the writing and publication of this book there have been two pilgrimages to Les Saintes Maries de la Mer. I was not able to attend, but the local paper (confirmed by eye-witnesses) reported a progressive decline in the number of gipsies attending, and attributed this to resentment at the intrusion of tourists and particularly the *cinéastes* who treat a series of religious ceremonies as a show got up for their amusement and exploitation. If this continues, the pilgrimage will lose its peculiar, not to say unique, quality.

In spite of many fruitless enquiries I still hope somebody

xi

will explain why it is only on the eve of St. Médard that the Rhône gives up the ghosts of the drowned, who flit about bearing will-o'-th'-wisp lights, trying to collect the memory of good deeds which will eventually bring them to Paradise. It seems possible that Provençal popular tradition, so inaccurately but often so poetically tenacious of the past, may here have preserved in Christian form the memory of some pre-Christian belief. The date in the calendar of Saints would explain why the annual ghosts from the Rhône became attached to the name of St. Médard, who all over France is also confused with an ancient rain-god.

I hope readers will pardon the discursive nature (involving some repetitions) of a very informal book in which I have tried to present unfamiliar matter readably.

1

A Word to the Wise

In a real and literal sense Mistral was a 'representative man' beyond any of those Emerson chose for this distinction. Followers of Emerson's friend, Thomas Carlyle, would have liked to see him received as the 'representative man' of the nineteenth century. With all due regard for his abilities, which are probably more respectable than contemporary opinion is inclined to grant, Carlyle on the whole represents chiefly his own prejudices and tantrums, and the rather awful 'morality' of a Scotch village. Mistral 'represents' modern Provence with a power and thoroughness and felicity hardly to be equalled by any modern hero whose main power over his fellow-men was the written word. Emerson, Thoreau and Hawthorne put together do not so completely 'represent' New England. And even for Scotland you have to add Sir Walter to Burns and perhaps Carlyle to them to make a composite but truly 'representative' man comparable with what Mistral is to Provence.

How is it England and America have half-forgotten him?— for except for a few experts or Provençaux by adoption he certainly is half-forgotten there. It was partly because I was so amazed by visitors to the Midi asking me innocently: "Who was Mistral?" that out of my semi-ignorance I project this book. Mistral *was* somebody. What is far more to the point, Mistral still *is* somebody, still inspires and influences the grandchildren and great-grandchildren of his contemporaries to an extent which no other writer of his time has achieved. He is to Provence what Marx is to the intellectual underworld and the materialist under-dogs; and it is because Mistral stands for the values Marxism destroys that his memory and his writings are to be loved and revered.

I

When, at the age of seventy-four, Mistral received half a Nobel Prize from people who, it is rather doubtfully said, couldn't read his books in Provençal, he became 'news'; and from 1904 until the outbreak in 1914 of the great war to end war, Mistral was translated, books and articles were written about him, literary tourists called on him. But he was never really in the fashion of the Anglo-Saxon intellectuals. Mistral was outside their experience, too manly, too popular, and therefore to be patronised. And, of course, he did not fit into the 'ideology' of the 'dalectical materialists'. Here and there were exceptions. Arthur Symons—and he is to be respected for this—after a first condescending cockney nod from the Olympus of the Alhambra Music Hall and Montmartre, suddenly realised he was in the presence of his superior and later admitted the fact. Leonard Bacon, who knew many of the eminent men of his time, has more than once recorded that none ever gave him the sensation of greatness which emanated from Mistral's modest dignity. Sir Theodore Cook realised his power. There were others: Augustus John knew the world of Mistral, and one man—the South African, Roy Campbell— really became part of it.

But in general we may say that in few cases has there been such an exposure of the cold indifference of the Northerners as in their inability to perceive the Provence of Mistral. Tens of thousands, hundreds of thousands of them, rushed through Provence on their way from the night-clubs of Paris to the gaming tables of 'Monte'; and saw nothing of it. And after all, why should they? From Mistral's point of view they were part of the enemy, the leaders of that 'centralisation', the profiteers of that mechanical exploitation of men by machine-worshippers he tried to avert. By a bitter paradox the region he laboured so long and so successfully to bring to awareness of itself, to live its own life in harmony with its own traditions—that region was made the headquarters of cosmopolitan plutocracy and its inane extravagance. It was the unconscious revenge of the 'Parisiens' for the aloofness of Mistral's Provence and its fight to maintain the life of its ancient past. True, if we think of what such places as Cannes, Marseille and even Cassis (particularly loved by Mistral) were in 1850 and what they are now, it is hard not to feel that there at least (as well as elsewhere) his Provençal tradition has suffered great reverses. Despite all which and more, the true wonder is that so much has survived, and how greatly that survival is due to him.

In the Place du Forum at Arles—known of old as the Place des Hommes, because the shepherds and farm labourers changed masters there yearly—is a large bronze statue of Mistral. When I got back to the Midi in 1947 I found it had gone, and was told that, like so many other French statues, it had been removed and melted down for its metal by the Germans. A year or two later I was astounded to see it back on its pedestal, and a bouquet of fresh flowers laid in front of it. The tale as told is that when it was learned that the Germans were stealing French metal statues, the Arles statue of Mistral suddenly disappeared. It had been removed and hidden by those who cherished his memory. . . . "But," I asked, "why did you not immediately replace it after the liberation?" My Provençal informant closed one eye and pressed the side of his nose in a gesture of delightfully innocent cunning. "Too many politicians," he said, "wiser to wait until they'd all gone home —to Paris," he added hastily. I give the tale as it came to me.

Artistically it is not a good statue. Mistral himself described it confidentially as a brick dropped on his head, but I believe he referred rather to troubles with bureaucrats about its site than to its shortcomings. But there once more the weather-greened bronze stands, and the new Reine d'Arles always lays her bouquet of flowers before it. I like to look at it when I am in Arles—and I am often in Arles—and with satisfaction. "Who was Mistral?" is almost invariably the visitor's question.

In Avignon, not far from the palace of the Baroncelli—kinsmen, it is said, of Pope Julius II (della Rovere, whose sculptured oak-boughs surmount the entrance) and ancestors of the late Marquess, one of the glories of modern Provençal poetry, stands another statue of Mistral, a stone bust on a pedestal. It is at the top of the Rue de la République in a tiny little *place* named from another poet, Louis Le Cardonnel, not of the *langue d'oc* but of the *langue d'oïl*, Benedictine monk, priest and dreamer, who was born in Valence, lived in Assisi and died in Avignon. . . . I stood opposite it, thinking of Mistral and Le Cardonnel and of how France alone of modern countries deserves poets, for France alone really honours them; while the ragged, ill-organised procession of the Félibrige Centenary stagnated or moved briskly to the sound of their frail *galoubets* (pipes) and soft drums. Most of the Félibres were in the beautiful old costumes of their regions, and as they passed the bust the men lifted their hats, and the horsemen of the Camargue raised their *tridents* in salutation. "Who was Mistral?" For once there was nobody to ask me that question, for everyone in Avignon knows who Mistral is and the foreigners present were guests who had been invited because of their admiration for him. Yet I have been innocently asked the same question as far east as St. Tropez, where a bronze medallion of Mistral let into the wall of the old castle miraculously survived the vandalisms of the German melting-furnace and demolitions; and as far west as Montpellier, when I have called attention to the quotations from Mistral cut in marble and displayed in the streets. One of them is the famous (in the Midi!) refrain:

> "Aubouro-te, raço latino,
> Souto la capo dóu soulèu!
> Lou rasin brun boui dins la tino,
> Lou vin de Dièu gisclara lèu."

(Arise, Latin people, under the cope of the sun! The dark grapes foam in the vat, and the wine of God will spurt forth!)

How true it is that the newspapers have taught us never to be interested in anything we don't already know unless they tell us about it! How few ask to be told what it means and why it was put up on a wall near the grandiose Arc de Triomphe of Louis XIV. How many remark with casual contempt: "Ah, *patois*, I suppose?" It is not *patois*, it is the classic modern Provençal of the Félibres, and it comes from a poem recited by Mistral himself in the Peyrou in 1878.

These things are so much a matter of common knowledge in the Midi that I should feel ashamed to put them down on paper, were it not that I am writing for the people of another culture and language; not for the few who know all about Mistral, but for these others who have scarcely heard of him but might be interested if one could only interpret him aright. I spoke of him as a 'representative man', and these anecdotes I have so far given at least show two facts—that Mistral was greeted with popular enthusiasm during his lifetime and that his memory is still revered forty years after his death. He certainly reversed the bitter saying that a poet is not without honour save in his own time and his own country. Other poets of other tongues have indeed enjoyed immense reputations in their lifetime—Victor Hugo, Tennyson, Longfellow, Kipling, Carducci—only to have them depreciated almost to nothing after their deaths, and very slowly and after a lapse of time rise to a less unjust valuation. This did not happen and has not happened to Mistral in Provence. If he was adulated and over-esteemed in his lifetime, there has been hardly any decline—only a few weeks before I write these words I heard him publicly referred to as "the greatest poet of the Occident"! It was a *galéjade* (a boast of the Midi), but though none of the three or four hundred present took it seriously, nobody objected.

The writer of a fairly recent life of Mistral called it (in French) *The Harmonious Life of Mistral*. I have not read the book, and I am told it is open to the objections usually made to any alliance of fiction and fact in biography, but the choice of the adjective 'harmonious' to express the quality of Mistral's life is not only exact and excellent—it is almost inevitable. It *was* a harmonious life, and his was a harmonious personality. Like everybody else he had his troubles, his dissensions, his disappointments, his regrets:

"Who never ate his bread in sorrow,
Who never spent the midnight hours,
Weeping, and waiting for the morrow,
He knows you not, ye heavenly powers."

Unless he had been subject to these sufferings of our human fragility, he would not have been a whole man. Indeed, genius from its greater range of feeling and superior susceptibility doubtless suffers more rather than less than other persons. But, upon the whole, Mistral's personality was that of a man eminently at peace with himself; and his life had the harmony of a long existence always in sympathy with its earthly surroundings and, above all, with its neighbours. It was an immense privilege, a great accretion of strength. We have become so accustomed to think of the poet as victim and martyr that, unless he is both, and is hounded to the grave by envy and misery, we begin to suspect he is not a poet. Is there an English poet, whose life is known as Mistral's is known, whom we could without irony call 'harmonious'? Tennyson, perhaps? But he lived for years in a cloud of literary spite and insulting anonymous letters; and, incredible to relate, instead of feeling contempt—or at any rate that mitigated repulsion we feel for the emanation of the skunk which can't help it—he was hurt. Think of the lamentable roll of English poets who by no hyberbole of affectionate straining can be called 'harmonious'; of the French poets of the north who have a most authentic claim to the '*poète maudit*' which Verlaine conferred on himself and on Rimbaud and Tristan Corbière, Laforgue, and how many more?

There was a serene, unhurried self-confidence in Mistral which is rare in human beings, rarest of all in poets. If we have read our annals right, we think only too justly of the poet fighting his desperate rearguard action with sickness, poverty, hatred and despair, hag-ridden by the sense that his time is short and he must hurry to express the genius that is in him before it is too late. Chatterton and Keats have become our ideal of a poet; but one who "lived out his life as the light"

6

must have something wrong with him. The artist as victim of mob sadism is so much a part of our accepted behaviour that an exception tends to strike us as abnormal—a condemnation which exempts only the octogenarian with one foot in Westminster Abbey, and the scions of Debrett who dabble in art.

A story, which has the rare merit of being true, rather neatly illustrates Mistral's serene self-confidence. There was a need for a new Provençal Bible, which seems strange when you think how many Protestants there were and are in the Midi—Nîmes is a great stronghold. Though himself a Catholic, Mistral thought that something should be done to correct this lapse. Surveying the task calmly, taking into account the vast amount of work involved, the fact that his time was fully occupied (his correspondence alone seems to have been formidable), and that he had not much time for translation with so much original work in hand, he made a characteristic decision. He would make a start, and hope that others would complete what he had begun. He and his friends the Félibres published a periodical, l'Armana Prouvençau (the Almanac of Provence) and each year at Christmas Mistral published in it the Provençal translation of a chapter of Genesis. At the end of thirty years he had done the fifty chapters, without any fuss or trouble he had given Provence a version of the whole book. I like so much that quiet determination not to be driven by a task, and the confidence that life is long enough for all we have to do—even to translate Genesis on the side.

The same unhurrying serenity may be seen in all the great works of his life. He was but a youth when he had that undefined but compelling vision—to which I must refer again —that he would devote his life to Provence. At twenty-three, with six of his friends, he founded the 'Félibres', the group of poets who were devoting their literary powers to the revival of Provençal, not as a patois as their opponents jeered, but as the living language of a people, successor to the Provençal of the Middle Ages from which so many of the forms of lyric poetry were derived. Though he was not the eldest of the group, the superior power of Mistral's personality and genius was acknowledged by all, including Roumanille, who actually had started the revival when Mistral was a schoolboy under his tuition. The *Armana Prouvençau* was founded as the periodical of the Félibres with a modest circulation of five hundred. Mistral and Roumanille raised it to ten thousand, and could say with some truth that they had made it the mouthpiece of the Midi. Yet, with all the applause of his friends and readers urging him, Mistral waited until, at the age of nearly thirty, he had perfected it before he published his first long narrative poem *Mirèio (Mireille)*, the work which made him known to the world as a poet and by which he is especially known in Provence to this day.

As I shall explain in more detail later on, Mistral 'serenely' avoided the dangers and temptations which awaited the author of a success so unexpected and so complete. Above all, he did not allow himself to be hurried into any effort to "follow up his success". Although his next long poem, *Calendau*, was begun before *Mirèio* was published he did not issue it until 1867, having spent seven or eight years in perfecting and polishing—some say, over-polishing—the poem; and he waited until 1875 before publishing his first collection of short poems, *Lis Isclo d'Or*, The Golden Isles, the three islands off the Côte des Maures, then almost unknown though now familiar to tens of thousands of visitors.

So it was with his other books. They appeared at long intervals, and only when he was ready to give them out. It has been pointed out, with perhaps a touch of cynicism, that Mistral was able to do this because he was the son of a prosperous farmer, and lived quietly with his widowed mother until his marriage comparatively late in life. But the modesty of his home shows that this prosperity was only relative. It was wisdom rather than an easy existence which persuaded him to spend almost the whole of his long life in the small village near which he had been born. And this leisurely production does not mean that Mistral lived the life of a literary recluse, like that magnificent writer but somewhat neurasthenic and pessimistic Norman, Gustave Flaubert. On the contrary, good fellowship and, above all, friendship and sympathy with the men and women who work with their hands were an essential part of Mistral's life and art. Obviously his Félibres were not the first group of poets or artists to enjoy convivial meetings and excursions, where the service of the Muses did not exclude due homage to Venus, Ceres and Bacchus. But so much of this aspect caught the public attention that the Félibres, particularly the exiles in Paris, were sometimes jeered at by the ill-natured as *farceurs* whose activities were limited to taking their wives on Sunday literary picnics amid a thunder of *patois*—speeches interminable, songs and verses!

Here we come upon a significant aspect of Mistral's genius, which was also one reason for the immense popular reputation and influence he enjoyed in the Midi for half a century—I mean, that the real theme of his writings is always Provence. Now, of course, there were other regionalist writers in other tongues at the time—for the nineteenth century was a great epoch of regionalism in Europe—but they were too often either mere cultivators of the picturesque, or political separatists. Mistral did not disdain the picturesque and his opposition to what he called 'centralisation' and the anti-Christian Republic was in a sense political. But he had larger views than mere opposition. And by 'Provence' he certainly did not mean an emotional abstraction such as more bellicose nationalisms created with Kathleen ni Houlihan, Britannia, Germania and Marianne. By 'Provence' he meant not only the sites and the ancient cities and hamlets, but its history and traditions as they remained still living, though often wildly altered in popular memory and imagination; above all he meant the lives and occupations of the people both of country and town which he knew and respected so deeply. It was the life and tradition of his youth, when mechanisation and the de-humanising influence of the machine and the factory were threats but not yet grim realities. He not only recorded all he had seen and experienced of that life, he tried to save as much of it as he could. And the remarkable fact is not that in Provence as elsewhere so much that was of inestimable human value has been destroyed or lost,

B

but that so much has been saved. And Mistral helped to save it.

The organisation of his Félibres and their 'movement' naturally made inroads on Mistral's time and energy. And his popularity involved him in ceaseless demands. He was in reality far more the Comte de Provence than the royalty who inherited the title. He presided and spoke at innumerable gatherings, from Barcelona to Nice. Every new volume of poems or book of prose in Provençal or the kindred speech of Languedoc had to have an introduction from Mistral. He supplied them as cheerfully as he gave contributions to the various small periodicals which asked incessantly for them. He answered innumerable letters, and with perfect courtesy received the many strangers who from curiosity or some better motive asked to meet him. After the Nobel Prize especially this must have been sometimes an affliction, in spite of all his good-nature and friendliness.

One might fill pages with a bare catalogue of his varied activities, some of which may come out in the course of this narrative. But there are two which must be at least briefly mentioned in this rapid introduction. After a lifetime of work Mistral issued in parts between 1880 and 1886 (he was then fifty to fifty-six) his great dictionary or lexicon of Provençal-French, *Lou Tresor dóu Felibrige*—the Treasury of the Félibres. It is a vast repertory, not only of philological learning but of folk-lore and all that concerns the traditions and occupations and beliefs of Provence. Fascinating as this work is for those who have made some progress in the study of the Félibres, it is by no means indispensable for the foreigner who wants a dictionary. Mistral's *Trésor* is bulky, rare and expensive; and all reasonable requirements are met by Father X. de Fourvières's *Pichot Tresor* (Little Treasury) which in my experience is a perfectly adequate Provençal-French dictionary and is published by the Collection de Culture Provençale; while the same author's *Grammaire Provençale* (Maison Aubanel Père) is all that is needed in that respect. There exists also— but it is hard to find—an excellent little book, *Floureto de*

Prouvenço written and compiled by Lieut.-Colonel E. Nicholson. It is useful to English-speaking readers since it gives the grammar and the rules of pronunciation from an English point of view (the difficult 'o' mute is carefully explained) and the book contains a selection of Provençal poetry and prose made by Paul Mariéton.

Having based so firmly on his *Tresor dóu Felibrige* the language of Provence, Mistral in the last years of his life established what might be called the Dictionary of Provençal Popular Culture—I mean the Museon Arlaten. He started the collection in 1896 with his own money, and in 1904 was able to extend it and to house it worthily with the money of his Nobel Prize—the best public use of that prize which has ever been made, for the Museon Arlaten is a collection of live, not of dead, things. I shall speak later at more length of this noble collection —in making which, by the way, Mistral was greatly helped by spontaneous gifts made by people all over Provence, who realised the unselfishness of Mistral's purpose as well as the interest and importance of the Museon for the life of Provence. It is true that the Museon is the most vivid and eloquent commentary on the writings of Mistral, but that is inevitable since, as I shall have to insist continually, the real theme of Mistral's writings is not Mistral, but Provence in its widest sense. True, also, the Museon's reconstructed scenes of Provençal life are based on episodes described in Mistral's memoirs of his youth (*Moun Espelido*)—but they were illustrated not because they happened to him but because they were ancient rites and customs in which he shared as a child and could remember in their ancient as well as surviving version. True, again, there are photographs, personal exhibits, pictures of his triumphs and so forth, to the glory of Mistral. But he did not put them there. They have been added—and rightly— since his death, in tribute to the poet 'Comte de Provence'. As to the 'life' exhibited there . . . but I must keep this for later on.

I incline to think that response to the Museon Arlaten is probably a fair indication of the visitor's probable capacity for understanding and enjoying Provence. When I say 'Provence' I mean the Provence of Mistral and the people, and not the 'Provence', however agreeable, of the bathing beaches at Juan les Pins and Eden Roc, of the Cannes golf course and restaurants and shops, of Nice or even St. Raphael. If the Museon seems merely quaint and 'amusing', a 'competent' exhibition of provincial rusticities—well, best get back to the car, and push on to dear old Monte. But if, as happens more often than one might suppose from the "Who was Mistral?" querists, some deeper response is evoked, then perhaps it is worth while adventuring a little further. There is so much to know, to learn and to enjoy, that half a lifetime is hardly enough for it all. I incline to be indiscreet and to go further. The denizens of 10 Downing Street, the White House, the Kremlin, the Palais Bourbon and so forth have not the slightest interest for me. I wouldn't walk across the room for the purpose of meeting any of them; in fact I would go to a considerable amount of trouble to avoid them.

To adapt the words of the poet:

> "They do not seem to serve a useful end;
> And certainly they are not beautiful."

But a *gardian* of the Camargue riding in his wooden saddle on his nimble grey horse, *trident* in hand, and his girl riding pillion behind him in her lovely costume of Arles—delicate as a figure of Tanagra; a weary shepherd tramping across the stony immensity of the Crau the last miles of the scores which he and his flock have covered on foot during their *transhumance* from the lower Alpine pastures; a fisherman of Martigues; even the less picturesque *vignerons* of Languedoc, the idle *pétanquistes*, the water-jousters of the little ports—all these are infinitely worth knowing. They are men not yet enslaved by the miserable fetich of machinery or made self-important by the perversity of mankind and the sadism of power politics.

It is Euripides who first thought of recording (in verse) that the expected does not always happen, but on the contrary the

unexpected—an example of that grave and sententious statement of the obvious disputed by nobody which illustrates the
Mediterranean love of *vérités de la Palisse* which existed millennia
before that eponymous hero of the trite was born. The words
of Euripides came inevitably to mind when to my amazement I
found a sympathetic if superficial admirer of the people of
Provence in—hold your breath—Dr. Arnold of Rugby. I
would have wagered almost anything that such a sympathy was
impossible. But what do I find in the fearsome Doctor's
Journals (I begin to think Lytton Strachey was mistaken about
all his characters) under date July 20th, 1839, when Mistral was
a *garnement* either running wild in the fields round the Mas dóu
Juge or cheerfully learning nothing but love of Provence under
the ingenious but penniless M. Donnat in the boarding-school
of Saint Michel de Frigolet. . . . what, I say, do I find in the
journals of the moral Doctor (who has probably done nearly
as much harm to England as Debrett and Dr. Adam Smith) but
these astounding words:

"Salon. We have stopped here on our way to Marseilles
from Arles, and I really never saw anything more romantic
than it is. There are tall trees, one very fine plane among
them, in the middle of the street, and under their shade is a
fountain playing, which makes a perpetual music—up
above is the cloudless sky, and the almost full moon, and
below, in full activity, is the population of Salon. They
crowded round the carriage, as there was some difficulty in
getting open the boot, and I could have fancied myself in
Spain to see their dark faces and eyes, their grave manner,
their white felt hats, worn alike by man and boy, and to hear
their Provençal language, which sounds much more like
Spanish than French, and is indeed quite as like one as the
other, and the old *fille* at the inn might pass for Spanish anywhere. But what a difference is made by good laws and
regular government; here all is peace and civility, while on
the other side of the Pyrenees all is blood and hatred."
(Stanley's *Life of Dr. Arnold*, Vol. 2, page 348.)

Dr. Johnson said he would love even a dog (which is saying a lot) if you called him 'Harvey', since Harvey had been kind to Pomposo when kindness meant something. No one who has ever suffered the affliction of an English 'public' school can possibly love Dr. Arnold, but I shall at least always respect him for having written that passage and having that perception. Whatever may be said against Dr. Arnold—and I believe he will be an exhibit in all the historical inquests on England's decline and fall—he was a 'competent' philologer. Notice he speaks of the Provençal *language*, not *patois*; and records that to his ear it sounded nearer Spanish than French. I don't know about Castilian, but Catalan and Portuguese and Provençal are nearer Latin than French is.

You will not see those beautiful white hats in Salon today, hats which seem to have been rather similar to that worn by Goethe in Tischbein's portrait of the great man in the Roman Campagna. The interest of the machine-and-money-Pistols was better served by making and selling them a cheaper and uglier article—so they were jeered out of wearing the better thing. The planes and the fountain are still there, but you will not really enjoy them as Dr. Arnold did—in silence. The streams of motor traffic coming up from Marseille and from Aix are forced to use the narrow winding old streets of Salon, and inevitably destroy the dignity and repose of the place. Why not a by-pass? Well, there are hundreds of towns in France which would be improved by such an addition—but such a work is costly, there have been wars and inflations, and thus we pay for them. Moreover, Salon has kept intact hardly any of those Baedeker-starred 'monuments' which attract the paying tourist and so awaken the historical and æsthetic sympathy of governments; though its old Château de l'Emperi and the collections of local interest housed there will attract those who know "who Mistral was."

The mention of Salon brings to mind an aspect of Mistral— and indeed of most Provençaux—which must always be kept in mind. Salon was the home of the Jewish doctor and astrologer,

Michel Nostradamus,* who was such a prodigious success in his lifetime. The King and Queen of France consulted and flattered him, and his memory long remained in Provence—very likely still does. Now, in the character of the native Provençal there is simultaneously the love of telling tall stories (*galéjades*) which the teller knows to be invented, and at the same time an irresistible propensity to believe them—a credulity which has been mocked by the writers of Provençal origin from Mistral to Daudet. Mistral's mother was a complete believer in the predictions of Nostradamus, and he has told with charming humour how she actually tried to get him named 'Nostradamus' and how the name was refused for registration both by the mayor and the curé. And though he tried to conceal it, the fact is that Mistral would very much have liked to believe in Nostradamus, and very probably did to a greater extent than one would expect in a highly educated man who was the friend of some the foremost scholars of his age.

Roumanille's famous *Curé de Cucugnan* (which has become universally known through the French adaptation by Alphonse Daudet) is certainly one of the finest examples of good-humoured laughter at Provençal credulity, but there is a little anecdote written by Mistral for the *Armana Prouvençau* which does as well. There was a man in the fishing village of Martigues who often had to go to Marseille, and when he returned the people of Martigues pestered him for news of the big town. One day on his way back he thought to himself: "Well, there isn't any news, so I'll give them a *galéjade*." And he had the whole population of Martigues listening wide-eyed to a tale about an enormous fish caught by the Marseille fishermen, so huge that they could not get it past the island into the inner port, the *darse*. Fired with curiosity the whole town began to run towards Marseille to see the wonderful fish, with even the cripples and the aged hobbling in the rear. Well, when they started out the Martiguais laughed to himself, thinking how nicely he had taken them in. But then as he found that everyone had gone he became uncertain, then

* He was born at Saint Rémy, near Mistral's home.

15

anxious. And as the cripples came by he said to himself: "If they're all going, there must be something to see." And he started to run with them!

Now, without any intention of being satirical, I can't help feeling that something of the same sort occurred to Mistral himself in handling the legends of Provence. With a population at once so imaginative and so credulous there are of course innumerable legends deriving from a varied history of more than two thousand years, from old towns and buildings and ruins, and curious natural sites. I think Monsieur Emile Léonard's monograph on Mistral and the scholars demonstrates that Mistral was in close touch with modern historical science, and knew perfectly well that the legends he treated of *were* legends. But for the purposes of his art Mistral necessarily had to treat them from the point of view of the characters in his poems, to whom of course they were true. I should not care to dogmatise, but I should not be surprised if in time Mistral did not come to give them more credit as history than they deserve.

An interesting example of this power of the legend occurs in the case of La Rèina Jano—Queen Joanna I. This Jano or Jeanne is the Joanna I (1317–1382) of history, Queen of Naples, Jerusalem and Sicily, Countess of Provence and Forcalquier. During the whole of her reign she did not spend six months in Provence, and her deputies harassed the people with taxes for her foreign wars. She is suspected of having at least connived at the murder of her first husband, brother of the King of Hungary. It is said that she secured absolution for this crime by selling Avignon to the Holy See for a quite inadequate sum which was never paid. In the end she was captured in Naples, and murdered by the Duke of Durazzo.

After her death Provence suffered greatly from the wars between the Duke of Durazzo and his rival Louis of Anjou, whom Joanna had named as her heir. For some inscrutable reason this not very engaging Princess is the only one of their ancient rulers remembered by the peasantry of Provence. The legends and stories of La Rèina Jano are a creation of popular imagination, and owe nothing whatever to the upper classes who preserved and embellished the memory of 'good King René', the last native Comte de Provence. Visitors to the ruined princely fortress-town of Les Baux will remember that the charming little Renaissance building in the valley below is called 'Queen Jane's Pavilion', though it must have been built long after her death. But all over Provence her name will be found attached to towers and ruins and old houses, even old trees. And the tales about her are numerous. Naturally it was the legend of Queen Jane which interested Mistral both as a poet and as the recorder of the people among whom he spent his life. There the reality was the popular belief, not the facts as established by historians. And Mistral's romantic play about her can surely be defended on the same grounds—it would indeed be a hardship if the writer of a poetic play were not allowed to put legend before history. In the admirable preface to that play Mistral has collected the names of picturesque monuments and places to which her name was attached by the people. One of the prettiest concerns a large piece of glittering rock crystal on a steeple in Sisteron—the people called it Queen Jane's Diamond. But at the same time he tries hard, with the aid of learned citations, to reverse the judgment of history. And he winds up with a hope that Avignon will put up a statue of her and will teach its children to "love God and Queen Jane". Like a good Provençal Mistral had fallen in love with her legend.

The other caution to be made is of a more humdrum kind, and here by a strange little coincidence Dr. Arnold's son, Matthew, comes to our help. Few English readers of Mistral are likely to overlook the fact that his relation to Provence as a writer is rather like a composite of the relations of Walter Scott and Burns to Scotland. As a human being Mistral seems more self-controlled than either. Obviously he must have had love affairs in his youth and he certainly did not disdain the comfort at table of one of the bottles of Provençal wine which were sent him in quantities by admiring wine-growers. But there is no hint of wine-bibbing or of any cutty-stool scandal.

Mistral's Latin moderation and wisdom preserved him from that ambition for wealth and social station which so unhappily wrecked Sir Walter's life. Scott is much praised for living and writing as a man of the world and not as the professional author he in fact was—and no doubt there is merit in this. But if he had respected his art half as much as Mistral respected his, we should not have to regret that one of the greatest story-tellers ever born in our island betrayed his genius by over-hasty writing and wasted his gifts on too many trite situations and conventional fiction-characters. As a story-teller in verse Mistral cannot approach the speed and bustle of Scott's first three poems—and he was not a novelist—and as a lyric poet he lacks the fire and passion and even the verse of Burns, however much he resembles Burns in carrying on and improving the traditional poetry of his country.

That is obviously the judgment of a foreigner and an Englishman, and no Provençal will agree with it. And here Matthew Arnold's warning about Burns seems appropriate. He says:

"The real Burns is of course in his Scotch poems. Let us boldly say that of much of this poetry, a poetry dealing perpetually with Scotch drink, Scotch religion, and Scotch manners, a Scotchman's estimate is apt to be personal. A Scotchman is used to this world of Scotch drink, Scotch religion, and Scotch manners; he has a tenderness for it; he meets its poet half way. In this tender mood he reads pieces like the *Holy Fair* or *Halloween* . . ."

And here I break off the quotation because Arnold goes on to say that this world of Scotch drink, religion and manners is not a beautiful world, but often "harsh, sordid and repulsive". Now, life is apt to deserve all those adjectives when it is not sheltered in academic groves or behind the solid walls of substantial money. Very likely the life of Provence has and had "harsh, sordid and repulsive" aspects, though they do not intrude at all ruthlessly through the medium of Mistral's idyllic and idealising genius. But the warning is salutary. If we cannot hope to read a poet so near to us as Burns with the 'tenderness' and enthusiasm of the Scotch, we certainly cannot hope to read Mistral with the feelings of the Provençaux. We acquire the language painfully and imperfectly; it is their native tongue. A thousand verbal felicities and subtle allusions escape us and delight them. All the fascinating 'folk-lore' and sites of Provence are part of their lives from childhood; we explore them with the naiveté and ignorance of the tourist. At the best we can only acquire artificially what to them is second nature.

These truisms are not intended to discourage, but merely as a warning not to expect too much too soon from Mistral and the Félibres. People who speak of modern Provençal as a *patois* seem to think of it as being as near modern French as Barnes's 'Zummerzet' is to modern English, and that, with a reasonable knowledge of French and some kindred Latin language, Provençal may be 'picked up' very soon. I must say I didn't find it so, particularly in the eloquent poetry of *Mirèio* and *Calendau*. And the prose, even when it is made intentionally as simple as possible, is not so easy and the very similarities with French are sometimes a trap. I give as a very simple 'unseen' for the reader who knows French to test himself the opening lines of a rustic tale by Roumanille, who, after Charloun Rieu, is perhaps the most easily accessible of the Félibres:

"Ero un medecin que n'en sabié long, car n'avié forço aprés; e pamens, dins Cucugnan, ounte despièi dous an s'èro establi, i'avien pas fe. Que voulès? toujour lou rescountravon em'un libre à la man, e se disien, li Cucug-nanen: 'Saup rèn de rèn, noste mège; fèbre countùnio legis. S'estùdio, es pèr aprendre. S'a besoun d'aprendre es que saup pas. Se saup pas, es un ignourènt.' Poudien pas li leva d'aqui, e . . . i'avien pas fe."

But the language difficulty is not the main obstacle to full enjoyment. It can be conquered with work and determination, and I don't doubt that most people are quicker at learning languages than I am. The main difficulty, I think, lies in what I have already tried to stress, namely, that the infinitely varied theme of Mistral's poetry is not himself and his psychology— as so often with modern poetry—but 'Provence'. If we know little or nothing of Provence, then we are bound to find much of Mistral rather remote or unexciting. It could not be otherwise in the circumstances. But then the joint exploration of Provence and of Mistral, the one constantly lighting up the other and making it more enjoyable, is the very essence of the experience. Why is it that among all modern English-speaking poets Roy Campbell has the highest admiration for Mistral and is certainly nearest to him? Simply because Campbell lived as a professional fisherman at Martigues, learned the language by ear not by eye, and the life of Provence by having lived it.

2

Mistral's Early Life

Frederi (Frédéric) Mistral was born on September 8th, 1830, at the Mas dóu Juge in the commune of Maillane.

Now, if we want to get a little nearer this Provençal life, even that commonplace biographical statement must be a little elaborated. I have already related how Mistral's young mother tried to get him named Nostradamus, and was defeated by the civil and ecclesiastical bureaucracy of the time. She fell back on 'Frederi', because it was the name of a little boy who had carried letters and messages for his mother and father during their courtship. The father, François Mistral, had been married before and by that marriage had a son and daughter. According to the strict tradition of Provençal families only this elder brother had as a minor the right to be called 'Mistralet'; the newcomer was 'Moussu Frederi' only. The patriarchal discipline of these homes was severe. The girls, for instance, never drank wine; nor did they sit at table with their father and brothers and the male servants, but took their plate of food as it was given them and went away to eat it. This difference of name to the boys marked the distinction between the heir and the younger son. Thus, when the master died, we find that the Mas and its equipment went to the heir; 'Frederi' and his mother took their portions, and retired to a house in Maillane.

Use of the word 'Mas', meaning an isolated group of farm buildings, is characteristic rather of Languedoc than of Provence, where it is limited to the lower Rhône Valley—in other parts of Provence they are called 'Bastides'. It is the Latin *mansus*, and the place name, Maillane, is said to be Latin also. According to the philologists all place names in the Midi ending in *ane* are Roman, just as those in *ac* and *osque* are

21

Celtic or pre-Celtic. Place names ending in *argues* such as Aimargues, Marsillargues, Baillargues (all in Languedoc) are said to mark the sites of Roman villas formerly under the jurisdiction of Nîmes. Among those to the east of the Rhône (which is the boundary between Provence and Languedoc) are Mezoargues, Meyrargues and Vauvenargues. The last two are so far east and so close to Aix-en-Provence that they seem to shake the 'dependence on Nîmes' theory; but they and all similar names are unquestionably Roman.

Thus from a single commonplace sentence we can begin to see how the boy was born into an area steeped in tradition and history. We can go further. Twenty miles is a reasonable day's tramp for a healthy lad or youth with a natural curiosity for exploring the country round his home. Draw a circle on the map with a ten-miles radius and its centre at Maillane. It is remarkable what it includes: Tarascon with its castle of King René, its legends and fête of the fabulous Tarasque and St. Martha; Beaucaire on the other side of the Rhône, with its castle belonging to the King of France, and its great annual water fair which brought trading ships from half the ports of the Mediterranean; Avignon, the papal city and fortress-palace, faced across the Rhône by the French fortress-castle of Villeneuve; St. Rémy with its Roman arch and imperial funeral monument; the ruins of Les Baux with all its legends and great names; Fontvieille; the abbey of St. Michel, parts of both Rhône and Durance and many an unknown ancient village. Above St. Rémy is the rock called the Lion of Arles (Lou Lioun d'Arle), which heraldic lion, according to Mistral, gave its name to the Gulf and not the town of Lyon or the 'lions' of the mistral. And only just outside the circle lie the town of Arles (more important than Avignon in its influence on Mistral), Cavaillon, and the great ruined Abbey of Montmajour where the ancient Kings of Arles and Counts of Provence were buried. There indeed was more than enough to stir the feelings and imagination of a gifted boy, in a Provence where the old people including his own father remembered the world as it was before 1789.

The child who was destined to give poetic life to the memories and traditions of a land where the very names of the villages are charged with history was also from birth closely linked with the life of his own time and the hard work on the land. The contrast in character between Mistral's father and his maternal grandfather, Estève Poulinet, is piquant. Both men were *meinagiers*, well-to-do peasant proprietors, owning their own homes and part of the rich agricultural land round Maillane. Poulinet was mayor of Maillane, an office which in France has quite as much civic dignity as in England but carries even more administrative responsibility. Here the resemblance ceases, and it is perhaps not too fanciful to see these two as embodying two types of universal as well as Provençal character—the cicada and the ant of La Fontaine's very unnatural history. Anyway, Mistral's father was not only a hard worker and disciplinarian, but a saver, whereas Maître Poulinet was, according to his grandson, a *"franc galo-bon-tèms"* — that is, a tavern-haunter and a spendthrift. When Mistral *père* worked in summer heat and winter wind, Poulinet was apt to slack off; where Mistral saved, Poulinet spent, though he had eight children, six of them girls. Poulinet would go off on Burns-like carouses with his friends until he had spent all his ready cash. When he returned, penniless, his wife would attack him with reproaches—how was he going to find dowries for their daughters? "Pretty girls like them can marry without dowries," he would answer, and then cajole and flatter until his wife had consented to "another little mortgage" on her property. It may be pure imagination on my part, but though Mistral the poet obviously delighted in this ne'er-do-well grandfather, I feel that the probity and respect for labour and good conduct of Frédéric Mistral the town-councillor of Maillane were just a little outraged by him.

The harvest is earlier in the Midi than in colder areas, and traditionally took place round about the Feast of St. John, the 24th June—a solar festival far older than Christianity. According to ancient custom, children, the sick and aged poor had the right to glean in the reaped fields. It must have been about the end of June 1829 that Maître Mistral, working with his labourers as they were getting in the harvest, was surprised to see a pretty young woman among the gleaners. He went up and asked her name, and she replied she was Delaïdo, daughter of Estève Poulinet. "What! A daughter of the mayor gleaning!" And she went on to tell him that when she or any of her five sisters asked their father for money for a little finery, he told them to go out and earn it. . . . There must have been at least thirty-five years' difference in their ages, but within a few months the girl had married him. Mistral, in his poetic way, presents the story as a charming pastoral—Ruth and Boaz in Provence. It may be so. Penniless May often marries monied January, but . . . anyway, she lived to see her son famous.

Mistral, the 'harmonious', was fortunate in so many respects, and in few more than in the fact that until the age of eight he lived uncontaminated by school—and even then his schooling was so deliciously incompetent that it had nothing in common with the 'conditioning' of later generations. He ran wild on his father's farm, evidently the pet of the family, and a handsome little lad liked by all the farm servants. In *Moun Espelido* he has left vivid word-sketches of scenes he remembered from those distant days. Two of them made such an impression on him that when, as an old man, he arranged his Museon Arlaten, he reproduced them with life-size human figures in the correct local dress in rooms which reproduced typical rooms of the wealthy Provençal farmer such as continued to exist until well into this century.

One of these scenes Mistral could not possibly have witnessed in his own case, since it happened when he was at most a few weeks old; but of course he must often have seen it in the lives of other children as he grew up. The scene in the Museon Arlaten differs from that described in *Moun Espelido*, where contrary to all probability Mistral "seems to remember" it as he was carried out by his proud young mother as soon as she was able to go out after his birth! In the Museon Arlaten reconstruction, he has placed it at an earlier date. A large— obviously too large—bedroom is seen entirely furnished with genuine Provençal furniture down to the smallest details. The young mother, dressed in the costume of Arles, lies ceremonially in bed with her baby. An old woman, nurse or relative, sits sewing by the fire, while four younger women, all in the costume of Arles, are grouped, ready to make the traditional offerings and wishes to the young child. The first brings him an offering of eggs with the wish, *"siegues plen coume un iòu"*—little one, may you be full as an egg. The second brings him bread saying, *"siegues bon coume lou pan"* —may you be wholesome as bread. The third brings him salt saying, *"siegues sage coume la sau"*—may you be as good as salt. The fourth brings him a large, old-fashioned matchstick saying, *"siegues dre coume uno brouqueto"*—may you be straight as a match-stick. No man is present at the scene; and the symbolism of the gifts to a boy-child is obvious, and certainly older than Christianity. Probably this very ancient and curious custom had quite dropped out of use at the beginning of this century, though it certainly was not limited to Provence.

The still more elaborate scene which Mistral has reconstructed in detail immediately beside the visit to the young child must have been witnessed by him every year, at any rate during his father's lifetime. Here again we see the tenacity with which the remoter population of Provence kept up ancient and pre-Christian rites, though this is one which our own ancestors preserved until after the Reformation, for it is no other than the ceremony of the Yule Log. It is a solar festival, like the mid-summer (Feast of St. John) kindling of symbolical fires which the young people jump over in turn to ensure the return of the sun. I have seen the fires of St. John flickering everywhere in the Tyrol in 1935, and jumped over by the children in Languedoc as recently as 1955.* There is one curious difference between the old English Yule Log feast and that of Provence, as recorded by Mistral—in Provence the feast is held on Christmas Eve, not Christmas Day, and it is *maigre*; i.e.,

* It is still so popular in Montpellier that special precautions are taken against the fires spreading.

there must be neither flesh nor fowl served. This may be due in part to the scarcity of butcher's meat in an arid land.

The reconstruction in the Museon Arlaten shows a room fully furnished with all the traditional furniture and crockery, and the table laid for the feast—there are even reproductions of the traditional dishes on the table. At the head sits the woman of the house, and beside stands a *gardian* of the Camargue in the costume still worn and carrying the *trident* used to round up the half-wild cattle. Two women in the costume of Arles (one wearing the cloak) and a shepherd in his smock complete the characters in this part of the farm kitchen. At an angle to it we see the ancient hearth with all its brightly shining copper cooking utensils hung on the walls. A girl, a young man, an old woman by the hearth, a child and a dog all closely watch the patriarch, the father of the family, as he drips wine on the burning log. Only the family and their house servants are present. Earlier in the day the woman of the house set all the others at liberty for the day, and gave each one these traditional gifts—a cake, a stick of nougat, a handful of dried figs, a cheese, celery and a bottle of dessert wine. The log which was brought in and lighted at the Mas must not come from a fig tree, but from an olive or some other fruit.

Mistral chose for his reconstruction of this ancient usage the moment when the wine was poured on the log, and the old man pronounced these ritual words:

"Alègre! Alègre! Mi bèus enfant, Diéu nous alègre! Emé Calèndo tout bèn ven. Diéu nous fague la graci de vèire l'an que vèn, e se noun sian pas mai, que noun fuguen pas mens!"

Which may be roughly rendered as follows:

"Joy! Joy! Dear children, may God give us joy! At Christmas come all good things. God grant us to see the coming year, and if we are not more, may we not be less!"

26

Instead of our ancient boar's head and barons of beef, or later turkey and plum porridge, the feast was lighter but more complex. There must be three lighted candles on the table (symbolising the Holy Trinity) and at each corner a plate with sprouting wheat—as they found it withered to nothing in the tomb of Tutankhamen, symbol of the resurrection of Osiris, the grain-god. The first dish was of snails, which abound in the Camargue, and indeed all through the Midi. In the season I still see old women sitting by the roadside selling them from sacks, and I have myself seen them served with the long sharp thorns Mistral describes. Then, as flesh and fowl were forbidden, came fried cod, and mullet cooked in a sauce with black olives. *Aiòli*, a mayonnaise heavily perfumed with garlic, was served sometimes with the fish, but more often with the snails. These were followed by cardoon and blanched celery. Then came thirteen traditional sweets, which probably had symbolical meanings forgotten even in Mistral's time, when they were supposed to mean Christ and the Apostles. These were: grapes kept in the attic; a light bread made with oil called *fougasses* (I see them in Montpellier every day); almonds and walnuts; pine kernels; nougat; little milk-cakes scented with fennel; apples and pears; crystallised fruits; pistachio nuts; quince jelly, with which were served dessert wine and liqueurs. There was a big 'Christmas loaf', which could not be touched until a quarter of it had been given to a beggar.

How much pleasanter that frugality is than the orgy of expense forced on us! Christmas was intended as a feast of the poor; our machine-life has made it a vulgar ostentation of the rich. What has the 'Miracle Mile' and all the rest of the arrogant display of wealth in common with the Child in the manger? I think of the *santons*, the small brightly-coloured terracotta figures of the Holy Family and the Angels, the shepherds and the animals, and certain traditional Provençal characters, like the old woman gathering firewood. You may see the ancient types in the Museon Arlaten, and at Christmas for a few francs you may buy almost the same figures from street stalls in Toulon and Marseille and other Provençal towns.

Mistral's childhood! These two scenes, so meticulously reproduced down to the smallest details, must have had a special significance among the memories of his childhood. Apart from the obvious links with his parents, they are perfect examples of what he valued so highly—ordinary events of life given significance and poetic charm by the observance of ancient customs and beliefs. Thus the daily toil of men and women, however hard and monotonous, became a life ritual passing through all the phases of the year, enhanced by traditional feasts and fasts, pilgrimages, dances, songs, local costumes—that 'way of life' which is so perfectly illustrated by the collection of the Museon Arlaten which Mistral himself defined as the *"musée de la vie vivante et de la race d'Arles."* What Mistral dreaded for his people was their enslavement by the machine, whether industrial, bureaucratic or educational. Whatever arguments of an intellectual kind were brought in to support this idea, either by Mistral or his friends, the real basis is sentiment, the intense love for family, for the traditional life they led, and through them for the Provence in which they lived. He wanted to save the happy world of his youth and childhood. But . . . was not Provence so idyllic because the Mistrals were prosperous? The life of Charloun Rieu, so admirably told by Marie Mauron, seems to indicate that for the really poor peasant of nineteenth-century Provence there were grim disadvantages.

This poetic view of life was stimulated in Mistral as a child by the influence of both parents. With nostalgic tenderness he has related how, as his young mother turned her spinning-wheel, she told the child endless stories of the legends of Provence or sang him the old songs. His father owned and read three books, the Bible, *The Imitation of Christ* and *Don Quixote.* There is no way of measuring the difference, but it must be very great, between the mind of one working man who in his brief leisure reads intensively a few books of the highest literary quality, and another working man who reads only journalism and catchpenny productions. Unconsciously he set his son a standard, and his stories of the Revolution and of his life as a soldier at the siege of Figueras (this must have been in 1794) had a genuine poetry of their own. In the afternoon of Twelfth Night, encouraged by their parents, all the children of Maillane ran out with little presents of figs and olives, or hay for the camels, to meet the Three Wise Men of the East on their way from Arles. For some reason the Wise Men always changed the road and went "on the other side of the mountains", so that the children came back disappointed, only to find with joy that the Kings had taken up their abode in the church. . . . Mistral has defended eloquently this imaginative pre-education:

"Nowadays our brutal system takes no account of the wings of childhood, the instincts of the opening imagination, the longing for the marvellous—which creates saints and heroes, poets and artists—and as soon as the child is born we start to wither its heart and soul with crude knowledge. Poor idiots! time and school, above all the school of life, soon enough teach the paltry reality and the analytic, scientific disillusion of all that once enchanted us." (*Moun Espelido*, p. 41.)

But then the world's rulers and the world itself want no more saints, heroes, poets and artists. They want docile machine-minders, machine-fighters, propagandists, inventors of bigger and better massacre-machines. Folk tales and old legends and songs start the child off wrong, and time is wasted in extirpating their influence. But then Mistral hoped to make them human beings, though that is perhaps begging the question. . . .

A more relevant question is: Did Mistral completely idealise the Provence of his youth, particularly of those first eight years whose memories must have been uncertain? He must have been well over seventy when he wrote the book, and it would be astonishing if he hadn't idealised his childhood and youth. Surely the remarkable thing would have been if he had not done so? Yet I think that on the whole it is a true picture.

29

The stories he tells of the crude practical jokes played on his childish innocence are not exactly out of Theocritus; and he could easily have omitted them. The adventures when he ran away do sound unlikely, but then he is careful to drop a broad hint that he is relating what the child *imagined* he did. On the other hand what he tells us about the life on the Mas is confirmed by other sources. It was true, for instance, that the farmer sat at the head of the table with his workers seated below, and that the signal to rise was given by the head carter closing his clasp-knife. It was true that in those days wheat was grown in the plain of Arles on a scale unknown today, and that the *gavots*—the mountain population of north-eastern Provence—were warned of the harvest date by criers, and swarmed into the plain to earn extra money to help them through the hard winter. The traditional feeding of these temporary emigrants seems strange to outsiders, yet it still goes on much the same at harvest time. Obviously the exact diet varied from farm to farm and from generation to generation, but Mistral's account is fully confirmed from other sources. Not, of course, as a child, but as a grown youth he often had the task of bringing the harvesters their frequent but frugal meals.

At seven in the morning they had a glass of wine, and a slice of bread dipped in oil and vinegar with anchovy and raw onion. At ten they had a hard-boiled egg, a piece of cheese, and watered wine. At one o'clock they came in for dinner of soup and boiled vegetables. At four they had a salad and a piece of bread rubbed with garlic. At night they had mutton or pork or an onion omelette. The *capoulié*, or chief harvester, poured out the wine for them. They were three to a cup. In some accounts, this diet was broken into six or even seven 'snacks', with less meat in the one big meal at night. Although it is not stated in any account I have read, the breaking up of the day by these frequent halts for refreshment had a very practical reason. The plain of Arles is most certainly in the sunstroke area, and the long sunny day of June–July is a severe test for hard manual work. There had to be frequent breaks so that the men could rest a little in the shade, and quench their thirst with water and wine.

All men who work hard in the heat and sweat abundantly know the craving for salt which is supplied by this diet, and the thirst that goes with it. Long afterwards, in 1888, Mistral wrote for his *Armana Provençau* a little apologue which he called *The Harvesters' Six Meals*, in which he defended them from the sneer of a 'fat bourgeois' who asked how they digested them all. The men's *baile* (foreman, in this case) picks up two clods of earth, puts one in his trouser pocket and tells the bourgeois to do the same. The *baile* then cuts a swathe with his scythe right across the wheat-field, while the bourgeois with his cane strolls after. At the end of the swathe the *baile* asks the bourgeois for his clod, which he produces intact. The *baile* then pulls a handful of dust from his pocket and says: "*Moussu, vaqui coume, en brandussant la daio—frin! fran!—li segaire fasèn la digestioun!*"—"Monsieur, as the reapers keep moving their scythes—swish! swash!—that's what makes them digest!"

Very naturally Mistral the poet felt that this 'education' on his father's farm was far more important than the formal schooling which he seems to undervalue, though he was a very successful pupil and student. In this he was not wholly just. Of course, in later life he denounced the State education directed by bureaucrats in Paris which allowed village schoolteachers in Provence actually to punish the children for speaking their own language—one of the rights Mistral believed had been specifically reserved to Provence when it became a fief of the crown of France. It is perfectly possible to be a poet without knowing how to read or write—there used to be many such in Tuscany and Sicily—but Mistral was a man of very wide culture as well as a poet of genius, and he owed that culture to his school and university training. There is much learning in most of Mistral's writing, particularly in the narrative poems. Indeed, the hero of his poem, *Calendau,* has been criticised on the grounds that a poor fisherman of Cassis could not possibly have had his knowledge of the history of Provence, or have been able to derive the name of his native village from the Latin word, *cassis,* a helmet! But the story of Calendal is not a realistic 'reconstruction' novel, it is an imaginative fantasy, using all sorts of Provençal legends, and it is easy to suppose that Calendal got his knowledge in some mysterious, magical fashion. The point is that Mistral used his immense 'cultural' knowledge everywhere in his writing, but he only had it because of his 'schooling'.

In any event, the 'schooling' that he dreaded for other children of Provence began mildly enough in his case. Indeed, if we may accept his memories literally, his first two schools were not very 'serious'. The first was the village school of Maillane, where he seems to have learned principally the art of playing truant—described in *Moun Espelido* with much humour and vividness. When his parents decided that this would not do and that he must go to a boarding-school, they chose one which had the merit of being near at hand and in picturesque surroundings, but from an educational point of view was a kind of Provençal Dotheboys Hall, though the boys were well fed and not ill-treated. In fact, the difficulty was that the head-master and owner was too often absent, trying to drum up pupils on a fallacious system of bartering the father's trade product or services for the boy's schooling, while the under-paid assistants allowed the pupils to spend far too much time playing on the thyme-scented little hills of the Montagnette.

One of the inexhaustible pleasures of reading Mistral and the many authors in his ambience, whether Félibres or not, whether they wrote in French or Provençal, is that of visiting some of the many interesting or beautiful places they have made use of in their imaginative work. The building which housed this first of Mistral's boarding-schools was an ancient and partly ruined monastery, with the attractive name of Saint Michel de Frigolet. *Frigolet* (in Provençal, *ferigoulet*) might be translated "field of wild thyme", or Shakespeare's bank where the wild thyme blows—not to mention the wild lavender and rosemary which smell like fresh incense under the hot sun. It is even said that the wine from round there has an aroma of thyme, though œnophiles are apt to be a little fanciful in their detection of subtle flavours beyond the perception of an un-trained palate.

Saint Michel de Frigolet was originally a sister house of the great Benedictine monastery of Montmajour, whose noble ruins may still be seen on a knoll—once an island in the marshes—beside the road from Arles to Les Baux. The main task of these monks was that of reclaiming the wide marshes surrounding Arles, which are now fertile fields. Unluckily, wherever the Roman armies went they seem to have taken malaria with them, and the Benedictines of Montmajour suffered severely from the disease. St. Michel was built among the thyme and lavender of the Montagnette as a refuge for the sick. It was to the Montagnette that Daudet sent Tartarin de Tarascon and his friends to shoot at their caps; and St. Michel was the abbey he had in mind when he wrote his story of Father Gaucher, the distiller of potent liqueurs for sale by the community, and the grievous temptation into which he fell. It is a good story, but a better is Mistral's tale of the Abbé Talon and his misfortune—which may possibly have suggested the story of Father Gaucher to Daudet, who had a great flair for snapping up other people's tales. M. Talon had been deprived by his Archbishop for "lifting his elbow" too often, and sent as chaplain to M. Donnat's ill-fated school. Leading the procession of the Fête-Dieu in a neighbouring village after lunch, the abbé scandalised the faithful by steering a zig-zag course in his embroidered cope. It was he who gave the authority of his rubicund countenance to the annual Pilgrimage of Bottles. Each man carried a bottle of wine, and when all had assembled in the chapel of St. Marcellin at Boulbon the Abbé Talon intoned joyfully:

"My brethren! uncork your bottles, and receive the Benediction in silence!"

He then chanted the formula which blessed the wine, the congregation said "Amen," each man crossed himself and drank, and the mayor and the abbé clinked glasses on the steps of the altar.

One of Mistral's happiest anecdotes of his father is connected with this remarkable school. Maître Mistral had a favourite mule called Babacho, known in every market town of the district, which he always rode when he went round his land cutting down weeds as he sat in the saddle with a long-handled spud. Well, in his second year at St. Michel, Frédéric wrote his father that he had started Latin and needed books. Some time later the old man arrived at the monastery school on Babacho, with a large saddle-bag from which—so his son says—he produced dictionaries, Latin books, a vast jar of ink, an armful of quills, and enough paper to last seven years, exclaiming: *"Frederi! t'ai adu quàuqui libre em 'un pau de papié'"*—Frederic, I've brought you a few books and a little paper!

Since those days the monastery has been re-occupied and repaired and greatly added to, twice evacuated by order of the anti-clerical Republic, always re-occupied. The services are well performed, there is an annual pilgrimage, and at Christmas the shepherds make offering of a live lamb as they used to do at Les Baux. But it is useless to look for Father Gaucher or the Abbé Talon.

This fantastic school in the ruined monastery lost in the thyme-scented hills of the Montagnette suddenly fell to pieces, as Mistral has related with his customary quiet laughter at the comedy of life. Whatever defects his school had, its care for decorum and religious exercises was zealous. And then one day, like thunder from a cloudless sky, came the news that the only female servant was with child, an immense scandal. She disappeared. The cook, who was strongly suspected as the author of this calamity, disappeared also. M. Donnat disappeared—nobody quite knew why, and his underpaid assistants packed their meagre baggage and followed. For a day or two M. Donnat's old, frail parents, left alone, fed the boys on potatoes. And when nothing remained but the peelings told them with tears that they must go home, which they joyfully obeyed in little groups making for their villages.

It was another date in Mistral's life, and henceforth his schooldays were passed in the streets of Avignon and Aix, where in those days the air breathed odours not of thyme and lavender, and the boisterous mistral was an alleviation. Avignon in the 1840s was not the clean, cheerful city we now enjoy. Viollet-le-Duc had not then restored its ancient walls which hung in crumbling ruins over a moat filled with fallen stones and rubbish and stagnant water. The streets were narrow and winding, the modern squares uncleared, the modern arteries unpierced. The Palace of the Popes was a barracks, and, worst of all, the political enmities bred by the Revolution, the Empire and the Restoration, followed by the Orléaniste coup d'Etat, had grown bitterer rather than milder, at least in words. After the Revolution of 1848 and the counter-Revolution of Louis Bonaparte in 1850, the political strife straggled into absurdities. With his genial laughter Mistral tells us of a Royalist in Avignon who had lost his hat in a street fight with the Reds, and went bareheaded (in days when all men wore hats) to keep a vow that he would never wear a hat until Henri V reigned.

Avignon and Arles are the twin capitals of the Félibrige, the centres of the revival of Provençal culture. It is hard to say which of the two was the more important, and perhaps unnecessary, and it was a purely personal feeling which inclined Mistral's affection to Arles. But Avignon's influence was decisive in the life of young Mistral. And if the poets were not born, they lived there. Twenty-seven Provençal poets, beginning with Mistral of Maillane, accepted the invitation of Bonaparte Wyse and his wife to the banquet they gave in 1867; and seven of them were from Avignon, none from Arles. It is a digression, but I wish I could allow space to give the reader the menu of that banquet and its eleven wines of Provence. Omitting copious *hors d'œuvre* and desserts, there were six courses and twenty-two *plats*—a Franco-Irish country gentleman in those days could afford a spread beyond the dreams of millionaires. . . . Anyway, Avignon and its Lycée made Mistral an intellectual—in one of his years there he took every prize in his class and the *Prix d'excellence* of the school. Let us not affect disparagement of that scholastic triumph—it showed at any rate that Mistral had a mind—but the wonderful thing, approaching the miraculous, was that in a change of schools in Avignon he had as a junior master—Roumanille.

35

Clearly this coincidence of the lad Mistral finding Joseph
Roumanille as a young master in his own school was of
immense importance to him. So far as is recorded, Roumanille
was the first living poet of the *langue d'oc* with whom Mistral
came into personal contact, certainly the first with whom he
was on terms of intimacy. But contact with the writings of
other poets is valuable and worth recording in the early
development of such a mind. Nobody can read Mistral without
seeing that Virgil and Homer were familiar to him, and of
course he must also have read the 'classical' French poets.
Probably at that time the school courses did not include
Lamartine, but in the 1840s it was impossible for any intelligent schoolboy to be ignorant of Lamartine, and his
influence on Mistral as a poet is as obvious as his generosity in
making the young man's reputation. Béranger clearly was not
an 'official' poet under Louis Philippe. With his customary
quiet laughter Mistral has recorded how one of his schoolmasters who "detested the English" would interrupt his lesson
to sing them one of Béranger's bellicose songs, beating time on
his desk, probably in the hope of stimulating his pupils to a
guerre de revanche. For obvious reasons the English were not
popular with the Bonapartists or any of the various types of
chauvins. In the Midi it was believed—and still is, for I have
heard the tale myself—that 'Nelson' wantonly burned all the
lovely pine groves of the island of Port Cros. Perhaps he did—
war is not an intelligent occupation—but there is an undoubted
myth about Nelson still believed, not only in the Midi but in
other parts of France. It is that Nelson was shot on the
quarter-deck of the *Victory* by a native of Provence, Robert
Guillemard of Six-Fours, who received a government pension.
No such person existed, and the name and episode are derived
from a short story written by a young Provençal lawyer of
literary tastes from Ollioules, near Toulon. But though the
myth has been repeatedly exploded it still persists. I find it in a
little *History of Provence* issued, it is true, under the German
occupation and passed by their censorship in 1944. Quite
recently a Paris newspaper stated that the French Admiralty is

still from time to time pestered with antiquarian researchers into the life story of this imaginary Robert Guillemard! I don't remember that Mistral ever refers to this story, but if he ever heard it we may feel sure he would have welcomed it with a laugh as one more example of that Provençal imagination which creates myths and the popular credulity which preserves them.

However much of a 'Classic' Mistral was—and it is almost superfluous to add that some critics have classed him as a 'Romantic'—the poets of the *langue d'oc* naturally influenced him most. Though he does not mention them among the poems and songs he heard from his mother, it is impossible to believe that in his childhood he did not hear either from her or others the Christmas carols of Nicholas Saboly and such popular songs as *Aqueli mountagno*, which is still sung by every child in the Midi. Saboly lived in the seventeenth century, though his poems have a naïve medieval realism such as we find in some English carols of the fifteenth century or earlier. The song *Aqueli mountagno* has a pleasantly simple old tune, and is a favourable example of the traditional *langue d'oc* song. There is a tradition that this song was written by Froissart's friend, Gaston III, Count of Foix, nicknamed 'Phœbus' because he was such a handsome and accomplished cavalier. Since Gaston Phœbus lived 1331–1391, this attribution dates the song to the fourteenth century, and the accepted version sounds much more recent than that, and much too 'folk' to be the production of a flower of chivalry whose main authentic literary work is a treatise on Venery. But of course such changes inevitably occur in any song or poem which is handed down for centuries by oral tradition. The song is so pleasant that I am tempted to quote it with a rough prose version:

> "Aqueli mountagno
> Que tant auto soun
> M' empachon de vèire
> Mis amour ount soun.

37

"Auto, bèn soun auto,
Mai s'abeissaran,
E mis amoureto
Vers iéu revendran.

"Avan dins la plano
I' a'n pibo trauca,
Lou couguiéu ié canto
Quand ié vai nisa.

"Que cante e recante
Canto pas pèr iéu:
Canto pèr ma migo,
Qu'es proche de iéu.

"A la font de Nimes
I'a un amelié
Que fai de flour blanco
Au mes de janvié.

"S'aquéli flour blanco
Eron d'ameloun
Cuiliriéu d'amelo
Per iéu a per vous."

(These mountains which are so high prevent me from seeing where are my loves.

High, they are high, but they shall be lowered, and my loves will come back to me.

Down yonder in the plain stands a hollow poplar, where the cuckoo sings when he goes to settle.

Let him sing and sing again, he sings not for me, he sings for my darling who is near to me.

By the fountain of Nîmes there's an almond tree, which puts out white flowers in the month of January.

If these were white flowers of the little almond tree, I'd pick the almond for you and for me.)

I give the version from the *Canto Jouinesso*, but another more logically in the fourth stanza reads "far from" instead of "near to". The vagueness of the poem shows how it must have been altered by passing through generations more interested in the tune than the words. If the original really came from Navarre and the mountains were the Pyrenees, then obviously the verse with its reference to Nîmes must come from the Rhône Valley. It doesn't matter, the song itself for all its uncertainties has a quite haunting loveliness. But will it survive a generation reared on Prévert and America's tin-pan alley? It is no doubt better dead than jazzed up.

If the origin of *Aqueli mountagno* remains uncertain, there is no doubt about the authorship of an eighteenth-century *langue d'oc* poem which had an immense vogue for many decades. Beside the Church of St. Roch in Montpellier stands the bronze bust of the Abbé J. B. C. Favre, author of the *Sermoun de Moussu Sistre* (which some think his best poem) and of *Lou Siege de Cadaroussa*. He was born in 1727 at Sommières, a picturesque old fortress town on the east bank of the Vidourle, where the still existing Roman bridge carried the highway from Nîmes. He became a good classical scholar, was at one time librarian to a nobleman, and held in succession several parish churches in the neighbourhood of Montpellier. He died at Celleneuve in 1783, and his Caderousse poem was first published in 1797. As an indication of its popularity we are told that in the last century the reading of thousands of homes in the Midi was mainly the poems of Saboly and Favre and the prose of the *Armana Provençau*. Mistral relates that one of his schoolmasters came from Caderousse (it is just to the north of Châteauneuf-du-Pape) and delighted to illustrate his lectures on Virgil with quotations from the Abbé Favre's comic-heroic poem, which is based on the tradition of an event during the famine year of 1709. The Papal Vice-Legate of Avignon sent to Caderousse to ask for wheat and, when it was refused, mobilised

39

the Papal Army (said to be about a thousand men with four guns) to attack the town, which capitulated and was handsomely robbed by the invaders. The fun of the poem depends so much on the skilful use of the language and on a knowledge of numberless local allusions that a quotation would not be of much help here, even the passage describing the intense indignation of the Vice-Legate when he hears the people of Caderousse *"Vous mandon umblamen fa fitre . . ." "Fitre!" repliquêt Doria, "Oh! Cadaroussa lou pagarà!"* ("They humbly recommend you to go and —— yourself." "—— myself!" exclaimed Doria, "Ho! Caderousse, you'll pay for this!") It is easy to see how such very broad humour would appeal to schoolboys and peasants. On the other hand, the allusions to Virgil and parodies of well-known passages would have amused the Abbé's colleagues at the University of Montpellier.

Mistral seems to have discovered for himself the poems of Jasmin in a newspaper; and in his enthusiasm sent him a schoolboy's poem of praise, which Jasmin ignored. Years later when the group of the Félibres was being formed, Jasmin snubbed them. Mistral has told us how much he was hurt by the old poet's silence, though he was too magnanimous to allow that or the later snub to modify his praise after Jasmin's death; but others were not so generous. Paul Mariéton remarks casually that Jasmin needed "only a little culture beneath his genial emotion" to be a classic. And his giving all the credit for the renewal of poetry in the *langue d'oc* to Roumanille is unfair to Jasmin, not to mention the fierce revolutionary poet of Marseille, Gélu, who had energy enough for half a dozen poets. Of course, if you limit "modern Provençal poetry" to that written by poets in the Avignon–Arles area, what Mariéton says of Roumanille is perfectly true. Ambiguity arises from using "Provençal poetry" as equivalent to "poetry in the *langue d'oc*". In spite of Folquet of Marseille and the troubadours of Les Baux, the poets of the 'classic' epoch before the Albigensian 'Crusade' were not, strictly speaking, of Provence, whose western boundary is the Rhône. Most of them came

from Poitou, Aquitaine, Gascony, Languedoc, and not from
Provence; and in the Middle Ages their language was not
called 'Provençal' but 'Limousin'. It is one of Mistral's glories
that, with all his love for Provence the ancient Kingdom or
Comtat, he laboured unselfishly to include in his movement all
the different areas where the *langue d'oc* is spoken.

For the native place of Jasmin, you must go, not to Provence,
but to Gascony, to the ancient cathedral town of Agen where
he was born in 1798. If you walk away from the cathedral in
the direction of the Garonne and the Promenade du Gravier,
you will come on the Place Jasmin, where there is a statue of
Jasmin and Jasmin's house. His real name was Jacques Boé,
and he came of parentage so poor that in his childhood he was
indebted to the succour of the Church. When he was old
enough to work, he became a barber, eventually was able to
set up his own shop, and attracted customers by the songs he
composed and sang, and modestly called *Papillotos* or 'Curl-
papers'. But though he had this gift of improvisation he
worked with unceasing care to perfect the poems he published.
In 1847 he noted that five poems which totalled two thousand
four hundred lines had cost him nearly twelve years of work!
He was a master of pathos, and his poem of Martha—founded
on fact—is very touching. So too is the story—not a myth—
of how he restored a ruined church, an episode which seems
much more like something from the Middle Ages than from
the prosaic year 1843. Without a moment's hesitation Jasmin
responded to the curé's plea for help in raising funds, and
tramped from town to town, singing or reciting to the crowds.
Among the songs was one in which he imaginatively foresaw
the ruined church rebuilt:

"And I shall say to myself: 'I was naked, and I remember
that when I was a little child the Church clothed me. Now
I am a man, and there is a naked church, and I want to
clothe it. Give, all of you, oh give,' and let me taste the
sweetness once of doing for Her what She so often did for
me."

And, moved to tears, the humble people of the Midi dropped their pence in the curé's hat, so generously that soon the church was rebuilt by a poet's songs. And the sequel is pleasing too. The church (of Vergt, an ancient bastide-town of Dordogne, on the road from Bergerac to Périgueux, not so very far from the castle of the bellicose Bertrand de Born) was re-consecrated by a Cardinal Archbishop, in the presence of five other bishops, three hundred minor clergy and a huge crowd. Jasmin, in the crowd, was overlooked, but just before the banquet the Cardinal told Jasmin he had heard of the new poem written for the occasion and "hoped Jasmin would read it to a few of us this evening." "Monseigneur!" said Jasmin, "do you think I laboured fifteen days and nights to make a little confidential talk? Today Vergt gives a fête for religion, but also for the poetry which understands and loves. Here the Church has six dignitaries, and Poetry only a sub-deacon. But he must sing his hymn officially or not sing at all!" It is said that Jasmin held the two hundred and fifty guests spell-bound with his poem, and that the Bishop of Tulle, who had to preach that afternoon, took it as his text. It is easier to smile at such triumphs than to repeat them. But unquestionably it was Jasmin who by precept and practice laid down two principles which still are the basis of modern Provençal poetry—that it should derive from the people and be addressed to them, that it should not be in any local *patois* but in a purified *langue d'oc* which would be understood throughout the Midi. Jasmin's error was in thinking that he was the last of the poets of the *langue d'oc*. Without knowing it he was one of the precursors of a great revival.

However important these influences in young Mistral's life, the time came when—without his knowing it—he needed the influence and guidance of a contemporary. These, of course, came from Roumanille, whom he might very likely have met later, since Roumanille's home at St. Rémy was near Maillane, and the parents of both knew each other. A curious series of little accidents led first to young Mistral being transferred to another school, where Roumanille was employed, and yet another to the revelation of their mutual sympathies and interests at just the right time.

It began, strange to say, with carrots. M. Millet was agreeable enough when he was cheering the hours devoted to Latin with amusing quotations from *Siège de Cadaroussa*, but his zeal for economy resulted in his serving his pupils too frequently with boiled carrots. This is not an exhilarating diet, and it is not wonderful that in his middle teens young Mistral began to feel discontented with Avignon, to wish he could hear the language of his native village, and to envy the very servants at the Mas dóu Juge who ate his mother's good bread. In this mood he read a newspaper article about the Carthusian monastery of Valbonne, which is situated at least fifty kilometres to the north of Avignon. Running away, it will be remembered, was a favourite sport of the schoolboys of Maillane. He would run away again, and be a Carthusian monk. And as he tramped the road northward, his imagination pictured him wandering among the trees, lost in the service of God, and at last becoming as holy as St. Gent. . . . And there young Mistral suddenly stopped. St. Gent, you must know, is a Provençal Saint, but an unofficial one—he is recognised by the people but not encouraged by the clergy, and his chief use is as a rain-maker. He obtained this power because he ran away from home as a boy and became a hermit. His mother pined for him, and wandered far and wide until at last she found her son's hermitage. When she arrived she was very thirsty, so the young saint touched a rock in two places, from one of which ran water and from the other wine. The wine has unluckily dried up, but the water spring still remains to prove the truth of the story. . . .

This recollection of St. Gent and his mother's distress suggested to Mistral that if he went straight on and became a Carthusian at once his own mother would never know what had become of him—he must go first to Maillane, and tell his parents about his sudden religious vocation. But the nearer he drew to Maillane the more he felt that his love for his parents was becoming stronger than his vocation. When he

43

got home late that evening his mother in surprise asked why he had returned before the holidays. "I'm homesick," he said in tears, "and I don't want to go back to fat old Millet who gives you nothing to eat but carrots!"

Well, next day he had to go back, but with a promise that after the holidays he should go to another school, where, as it happened, Joseph Roumanille was one of the junior masters. Like Mistral he was the child of peasants, but whereas the Mistrals were comparatively wealthy farmers, the Roumanilles were 'poor gardeners', of Saint Rémy, an old town famous for its Roman monuments and for the neighbouring hill called the Lion of Arles. There is a hamlet called 'Roumanille' close to Saint Rémy, from which no doubt the family derived its name. The belief in the Mistral family was that they had once been aristocrats, and that the fine old house still existing in Saint Rémy and then called 'Queen Joanna's Palace' (Palais de la Rèino Jano) was really the ancient home of the Mistrals. Roumanille's father, like Mistral, had served in the French Army. According to him he had won the Cross of the Legion of Honour at Waterloo, but did not trouble to claim it after the defeat; and when the honour was conferred on his son, the old man remarked: "The father won it, the son wears it!"

Joseph Roumanille was a delicate child, and owed his life to his mother's devoted care, which he repaid by deep filial love. He was the eldest of seven children, and it is nowhere explained how it was that a couple represented as so poor were able to give their son a good education. But the fact is that they did. After the elementary school of Saint Rémy, Roumanille went to the college of Tarascon, where he became known for translating Virgil and Homer into Provençal. Later he went as assistant master to a school at Nyons, where the headmaster was the poet, Charles Dupuy, who transferred the school to Avignon just in time to receive as pupils Frédéric Mistral and the future poet and Félibre of Châteauneuf-du-Pape, Anselme Mathieu.

It was Roumanille's fate to win recognition as a poet first, then as a prose writer to eclipse his own poetic reputation, and finally to be remembered as much for his work as predecessor and organiser of the Félibrige and the poetic tutor of Mistral. It was a tutelage from which Mistral and most of the other early Félibres soon escaped, at least in some respects. With all his genuine tenderness and gift of laughter Roumanille had a narrow conception of poetry as social action in the service of the people, he was a militant reactionary in politics, and he was a prude. It made difficulties later on.

The story of how Roumanille discovered his pupil's interest in Provençal poetry adds one more link to the chain of coincidences which brought them to the same school. M. Dupuy's pupils—or some of them—formed part of the choir in the Église des Carmes, and it was Roumanille's job to see that the lads behaved themselves. During Vespers one Sunday evening Mistral's thoughts wandered a little, for it suddenly occurred to him that it would be a good idea to translate into Provençal the seven penitential psalms. He began with the text: "Purge me with hyssop, and I shall be clean: wash me, and I shall be whiter than snow," which he wrote down almost literally yet in excellent Provençal verse:

"Que l'isop bagne ma caro,
Sarai pur; lavas-me lèu,
E vendrai pu blanc encaro
Que la tafo de la nèu!"

At that moment Roumanille arrived with disciplinary zeal, and confiscated the paper. Expecting some schoolboy ribaldry or a note to a girl, he was astonished by what he read, and after church took Mistral for a walk on the old ramparts. "So you like to write verse in Provençal, Mistral?" he said. Mistral, said yes, he did, sometimes; and then Roumanille began to recite some of his own poems. Mistral has told us which they were, and on re-reading them I marvel a little that he was so much impressed, they seem so conventional and ordinary beside his own work. But then he was still only a schoolboy, and this was his first living poet who had the merit of taking

45

his own work seriously and of trying to make real poems of the life he knew, instead of the everlasting coarse jokes in rhyme which were then considered all the *patois* was fit for. Roumanille's insistence on the need to get rid of vulgarisms of speech was of the utmost importance to the younger and greater poet, who came gradually to hope that part of his life task would be to create a modern Provençal from all the dialects, as Dante had created Italian.

3

Before 'Mireille'

About two years after this mutual discovery of Mistral and Roumanille, Mistral completed his course at the Lycée of Avignon. This was in 1847, just before his seventeenth birthday, and there hung before him the test of the Baccalauréat, which in those days was conducted for the students of the region by professors from the Faculty of Montpellier in the ancient and pleasant town of Nîmes. Perhaps Mistral never wrote in prose anything quite as perfect as Roumanille's *Curé de Cucugnan*, which even Alphonse Daudet—the Parisianised exploiter of Provence and the Félibres—could not spoil in his French adaptation. But he was unquestionably an excellent prose-writer, and his narrative of how he took his Baccalauréat in Nîmes in the late summer of 1847 has an almost Biblical simplicity, directness and vividness, with the added grace of laughter which visited not the inspired of Iaveh.

A journey alone from Maillane to Nîmes (it must be quite thirty-five kilometres), a couple of days alone in a great town, the task of satisfying the fearful curiosity of the yellow-gowned professors of Montpellier—here were terrors which Mistral unfeignedly admitted to his father, who bade him remember the famous seige of (not Caderousse but) Figueras. And gave his son 150 gold francs, with the sage advice not to waste or lose them. And his mother put up two freshly-ironed shirts in a handkerchief, folded and neatly fastened with four pins. And they kissed him, and he set out for Nîmes. And when he got there, he found he was a nobody, for nearly all the other candidates arrived with well-dressed parents, bearing letters of introduction and requests for favourable marking, from préfets and prelates and heads of universities and such

47

great men. All these candidates were certain they would pass, no matter what they did. And then came the written exam.

When he had done his best, young Mistral went out into the streets of Nîmes with his neat bundle and said to himself that he must find an inn which was not too dear. The more he wandered the streets, the more he felt intimidated by the hotels with their waiters in evening dress and supercilious airs. But at last he came on a real inn, which was used by the market-gardeners who came to the Nîmes market, and with them he could sit down and be at ease—until they asked him what vegetables he grew, and were astounded to hear that he was up for his Baccalauréat. So much so, that they agreed to wait and hear the result of his Oral.

When he returned for the Oral, Mistral found he had passed the written exam, and that a large number of those who had confided so much in their recommendations had not passed. Then came another of the meetings which are such curious coincidences in Mistral's life. The Professor who examined him, who had never heard or seen him before, was Saint-René Taillandier, destined only a few years later to be one of the most distinguished defenders of Mistral and the Félibres.

Mistral found he had passed. And here comes a very nice touch, revealing the simplicity and innocence in which Mistral had been brought up. When he left the examination room, walking indeed on air in his delight at having passed, he found that he was very thirsty, and that he was looking enviously at the people in the cafés drinking cool beer. But he had never been in a café, and in spite of his thirst was afraid to enter (in spite of the six gold pounds in his pocket) and quenched his thirst at a public fountain. When he got back to the little inn, the gardeners and the hotel servants saw at once from his lofty tread that he had passed. And the chief of the gardeners wept a little, and requested that he might speak, and said:

"O son of Maillane, we are all happy! You have showed these town people that the earth breeds men as well as ants. Girls! Join hands, and a *farandole!*"

And, says Mistral, they joined hands and danced a *farandole.*

48

Eight and fifty years had passed when he came to write down that scene, and he tells us that whenever he went to Nîmes thereafter and saw the sign of that little inn he remembered those two days, and "I think with pleasure of those good people who first taught me the good-tempered simplicity of the people and the joy of popularity."

The question may be asked: How far is this pretty story true? Obviously, without the omniscience of a deity nobody can answer that definitely. I should say myself that the event is seen through the perspective of time in the golden glow of youth, that strict realistic accuracy (e.g., the number of days occupied by the exams) is not observed, and that the long discussions with the gardeners (which I have not quoted) are certainly not intended as a verbatim Boswellian report. But the essence of the thing and such details as the lad's shyness about entering a café, the pleasure of the gardeners in his success, the *farandole*, are surely true. It seems to me that this is quite in the key of *Moun Espelido* throughout—an essentially true narrative is given an idyllic tinge. This is really what he did in *Mireille*, in the sense that the life of the Camargue and the Crau is exactly depicted but with an idyllic touch. *Calendau*, *Nerto*, the *Rhône*, and *La Reine Jeanne*, are all more romantic and fantastic, intentionally so—the prodigious deeds of the Cassis fisherman, the Drac of the Rhône who can transform himself into a young Prince of Orange are purely imaginative creations.

There is another aspect to this Nîmes story which should be noted. The complete unaffected sympathy between young Mistral and these gardeners and hotel servants is not a very common experience of writers. You cannot really become one with the agricultural population by running down to the country for the week-end and standing beers to rustics in the pub. And a genuine mutual sympathy between a writer and the industrial population must be even rarer. D. H. Lawrence knew his Midland coalminers as Burns knew his Scottish peasants, because he was born one of them; just as Mistral was born one of the farmers of Provence. But how soon a higher education and the beginnings of literary success made a breach!

In more than one of his earlier stories Lawrence has faithfully
recorded the breach between himself and his working-class
friends. But what could he expect when he had married an
aristocrat and had made friends with the family of the reigning
Prime Minister? He couldn't then go on being Bert the miner's
kid. Something of the kind happened to Mistral, but less
harshly, for everything in his life seemed to move 'har-
moniously'. Rather wistfully he has related how when he
returned to the Mas after seven years of school he found he was
no longer accepted by his contemporaries as wholly one of
themselves. The other boys and girls of his age understood
each other completely, but with him they were reserved.
Mistral could no longer unfeignedly share with the youths of
his age their admiration for a fine yield of wheat or a strong
willing mule or a neatly piled dung-hill. The girls were on
their guard with him, thought of him as a 'monsieur', and he
was convinced that not one of them would have listened to
him if he had made love to her. And somebody has remarked,
not unkindly, that eventually even his parents saw that Frederic
wrote too well about the farm ever to be able to work it
successfully. And a few pages later in his memoirs Mistral, all
unconscious of the social distance travelled, is telling a little
anecdote about himself and His Royal Highness, the Duc
d'Aumale!

There is a difference between being a poet who writes
authentically of the people, and a poet who is accepted by the
people. Mistral certainly was the former, but was he really the
latter too? In spite of his immense prestige and influence, it
seems that Mistral was not truly popular as Jasmin and
Charloun were in the Midi, and Burns in Scotland. Everyone
in Provence knew the story of *Mirèio*, everyone could sing the
song of *Magali*; but then *Magali* was 'folk' before Mistral took
it up and made it a masterpiece, as Burns did with the traditional
Scottish songs. To be accepted by the people it is not enough
to interpret the life of the people with knowledge, or even with
genius. Most readers of English poetry will agree that the life
of the English peasant has seldom been better or more sincerely

expressed than by the Dorsetshire poet, William Barnes. Yet when he was brought to Hampshire to lecture to the people and to recite his poems, the audience thought he "was flat after the paid entertainers" to whom they were accustomed.

Part of the 'harmony' of young Mistral's life came from his excellent relations with his parents, with his old father as well as with the young mother who, wearing her Provençal costume, received her son's prizes and laurel wreaths so calmly but happily at the prize-giving. Certainly, Mistral lived in awe of the patriarch who ruled his family and workers with such unquestioned authority, but Maître François seems to have felt great tenderness for this child of his old age and to have treated him with exceptional understanding. As the farm went to the elder son, it was the natural and traditional thing for the younger son to receive an education for the Church. But apparently no pressure was applied when Mistral began to show that he had no vocation, and, what is more remarkable in a peasant-proprietor, he does not seem to have opposed but rather to have favoured his son's natural gift for poetry.

After Frédéric had taken his Baccalauréat, Maître François allowed him a year at home. Doubtless, Frédéric was ex-pected to take his share of the farm work, and we have already seen that at harvest time it was his job to take the harvesters the food they ate during their rest periods. But he seems to have had an easy time, with all the leisure he needed for his studies and his writing; and it is well to remember that the 'studies' were not confined to books, but included the people who came to work on the Mas and all they had to tell about their own lives and the life and traditions of Provence. They were the inspiration of his first long poem, called *The Harvests* (*Li Meissoun*), composed between Mistral's seventeenth and eighteenth birthdays and never published. The extract given in the *Isclo d'Or* under the title of *La Bello d'Avoust* seems to have been a poem introduced into the main work, which was intended to describe the Provençal harvest along the lines of Virgil's *Georgics*. *La Bello d'Avoust* is in quite another key, being the story or ballad of the fair Margai de Vau-Meirano, who finds that the lover with whom she elopes is no other than the Demon himself and the wedding feast was in Hell. What this had to do with the harvest is hard to say, but it may be some old legend of Les Baux which was recited by one of the harvesters. The few lines of the main poem quoted are too few for one to say anything about it. Mistral says the poem was in four cantos, but as he later speaks of its "thousand lines" they can't have been very long. *La Fin dou Meissounié* is dated 1853, but may derive from the older poem.

While young Mistral was thus peacefully engaged, Provence, like the rest of the world, was startled to hear in February 1848 that there had been another revolution in Paris, and that the Orléans family had followed the Bourbons into exile. Revolutions, almost any kind of innovation, have a fascination for the young, and there is nothing surprising in the fact that Mistral at once became (aged seventeen) an enthusiastic supporter of the new republic. In this state of pleasant excitement he wrote in French a poem proclaiming eternal war on kings, which was reproduced in several newspapers. Not content with this he joined one evening with other youths of his age and sang the *Carmagnole* with them while they waved their red belts as revolutionary banners. This was too much for Maître François, who had vivid memories of the violence and disorders of the first Revolution, and he drew his son aside into the fields to remonstrate. "What," he asked, "have kings done to you, Frederi, that you want to kill them all?" Taken aback by this, Mistral could think of no cogent answer, though he defended his cause as well as he could from the old man's criticism. By June of 1848 Maître François was so far justified that the disturbances caused by the revolutionaries had troubled the whole nation, and the naïve hopes of the early days were already lost in the wretchedness of endless political strife. Even a village like Maillane was affected. Whereas before the revolution everyone had been cheerful and friendly with no thought of politics, they were soon divided into Reds and Whites. The Whites wore green ties and belts, the Reds their own colour; the Whites carried fleurs-de-lys, the

Reds thyme; the Reds planted trees of liberty, and the Whites cut them down at night; which led to fights and stabbings. For a time the Provençaux, who had spent their leisure in friendly gatherings and feasts, were turned into wrangling political sectaries.

How long Mistral was in recovering from this attack of political scarlet fever we are not told, but apparently it did not last long if we can take literally what he said to a friend fifty years later—that he had entered the local Council in 1848 and as a Monarchist! Apparently in the 1890s he still sat as a more or less platonic Monarchist, certainly no royalist fanatic like a few of his followers of the Charles Maurras kind.

Before the year 1848 was out, Maître François had decided to send Frédéric to follow the three-years course in Law at the University of Aix-en-Provence. It may have been his poem on the Harvesters which, as already mentioned, convinced his parents that he was better fitted to write about a farm than to manage one. And as he had no urge to take holy orders, the Law was for them the next best profession.

Not very much is recorded of the three years spent at Aix, and most of Mistral's recollections of the period are made up of anecdotes about his friend, Anselme Mathieu (1828–1895), who had been a school friend at Avignon and later was one of the seven original Félibres. He came from Châteauneuf-du-Pape and was noted for his eccentric behaviour and for the stories he told about supposed love affairs, which earned him the title of the "Félibre of Kisses". When he was going on for fifty he lost most of the money his parents had left him, and for a time kept the Hôtel du Louvre at Avignon. On the death of his wife, he lived in humble retirement until his death at Châteauneuf-du-Pape. But in the Avignon days he was full of life and fantasy, and was with Mistral on the students' outings, which extended as far as Toulon.

Mistral was twenty-one when he took his degree in Law, and returned home to make the announcement. The scene as he describes it is interesting. He arrived home just as the evening meal had been served, and before all the labourers had to stand and give an account of what he had achieved to his father, who said:

"Now, my boy, I've done my duty. You know more than I was ever taught. You must choose your own way in life—I leave you free to choose."

It was then that Mistral, standing on the threshold of his home and looking towards the Alpilles, felt vaguely but strongly what that future way would be—to make Provence live again through the cult of its own language and the prestige of poetry.

Mistral himself has warned us not to take this too literally, as if at that moment he had foreseen the whole of his future life-work. It was an emotion rather than a plan, or rather a complex of emotions. As a child he had been perplexed and even angered when his parents were especially deferential to someone who could not speak Provençal, a '*Moussu*', a '*Franchiman*'. Were the people of the Midi treated as inferiors because they spoke another Latin language? Well, the farmer's son with his *patois* had entered the *Franchiman's* Lycée and had walked off with every prize. Without much difficulty he had taken his Baccalauréat and a Law degree. In 1851, on the verge of the Second Empire, only sixty years had passed since Provence had lost its ancient rights and privileges and local government to the régime centralised in Paris. Moreover, another invasion of the north was beginning. After the destruction wrought by Charles Martel, the brutalities of the Albigensian 'Crusade', the wars of religion, Richelieu's demolitions, the *dragonnades*, the Terror, the northern industrial-capitalists with their servile State of obsequious politicians seemed about to move in and destroy an ancient civilisation in the name of 'Progress' for their own profit. And their standardised 'education' menaced the existence of his own language. What could be saved? How could the life and language of Provence adapt itself to the new conditions without losing its ancient virtues and age-old customs and beliefs?

Unlike the Catalans, Mistral and the Félibrige, while eager to save for the people all the unbought inherited 'way of life' which gave meaning and savour to their days on earth, were not devotees of archaism, always looking back and regretting the past. They fully understood that there must be change and new ways. The costume of Arles, to take a concrete instance, was never fixed once and for all, but had always to some extent adapted itself to the reigning fashion. Thus, the girls were not ashamed to wear it, and felt they were wearing clothes, not fancy dress. Whether formulated in so many words or not, Mistral wanted to save his people from commercial exploitation, which too often was the real meaning of 'Progress'. Centralised government, he thought, meant standardised people, and 'national education' was supported because it was an aid to selling them machine-made products—people who can't read were almost immune to the plague of advertising until the modern abuse of the loud-speaker. There was a genuine 'poetry' of the people which Mistral was not alone in thinking brought them more genuine happiness than the commercialised substitutes of the town. All said and done, the Church, whatever its faults, was to him a surer guide than the Bourse and the toe-ers of the Party Line. Whether so formulated or not, his life-task as he caught a glimpse of it on the threshold of the Mas was to be a defence of living values against mechanical, bureaucratic, statistical values.

How soon after his return from Aix and this flash of self-knowledge Mistral began *Mirèio* we are not told. But it cannot have been long, since the Museon Arlaten owns a profile drawing of him, dated 1852, on which he has noted that it was made when he was twenty-two and "had begun *Mirèio*". The very name came to him from his home, for though the original owner of the name was forgotten, Mistral's maternal grandmother used it as a name of affection for her daughters when she was pleased with them. And Mistral goes on to tell us of the other influences—far indeed from books and school and university—which went to the making of his first and in some ways most attractive long poem.

There was the Mas itself with all the life of the Provençal fields going on around it—the girls who came haymaking,

55

gathering olives, picking the grapes, helping with the harvest, bringing in mulberry leaves for the silk-worms. There was his own father, who is the model for all Mistral's patriarchs, and the shepherds, cattlemen, carters and others who worked for him. Among these was his cousin Tourrette, who had been a drum-major in the National Guard in 1815, and had convinced himself that he had tried to arrest Napoleon on the way from Elba to Waterloo. Cousin Tourrette had been little more successful in civil life, and picked up a poor living by doing odd jobs all over the Camargue and the Crau, but also gained a knowledge of the region which he retailed in picturesque language by the fireside at Christmas, kept by him with all the piety of a poor relation. The village girls used to hire him to tell them stories as they worked by candlelight, and he aspired to but never achieved the perfect job for a retired soldier—he had heard there was a good salary paid by Marseille warehouses to a reliable man who would sit in an arm-chair and count the dried cod-fish as they were carried in by the dock labourers. Evidently, young Mistral was not only delighted by this relative, but learned much from his tales and recollections of the Arles district. And there were other unconscious helpers: a woodcutter who had a lifetime's knowledge of the Rhône and its ways; and a peasant botanist who knew the Provençal names of the local plants and flowers and their supposed healing qualities.

With his half-laughing, half-serious belief in Nostradamus,* Mistral liked to feel that his life-work fell naturally (or supernaturally?) into seven-year periods. If *Mirèio* was begun in 1852, "one evening, at seed-time, when the ploughs were at work," its publication in 1859 exactly rounded out a period of seven years. Naturally, the creation of his poem was not the only event of those years. The most important in Mistral's private life was the death of his father in 1855. In his amusing parody of an Army furlough paper the old man gave his age as twenty-two at the time of the siege of Figueras. If we take this

---

* It must be admitted that some of Nostradamus's predictions were uncannily accurate.

literally he was born in 1772, and was therefore about fifty-eight when Frédéric was born, and eighty-three at his own death. It is sad to think that he did not live a few years longer to see the triumph of *Mireille* and the sudden literary fame of the handsome younger son of whom he was evidently so proud and whom he had so carefully educated. But he was worn out by his long life of farm labour under the fierce summer suns and winter mistrals of Provence. Two years before his death his sight had failed, and his last Christmas—which festival he had kept so merrily for so many years—was sad and silent. He ate the traditional dishes as his wife presented them, but all he said was: "Last year I could still see a faint glow from the candles, but now I see nothing." Life was no longer worth living—it was time to go in peace.

His father must be counted as one of the most important elements in the 'harmony' of Mistral's life. It is true that the character of Maître Ramon in *Mirèio*, evidently based upon Maître François, is shown as proud, stern and obstinate in his opposition to what he thinks a *mésalliance* for his child. We are not told whether there was ever any disagreement between Mistral and his father over a love affair, as there is between Mireille and her father in the poem. It is not very safe to draw such inferences from a poem! And the portrait Mistral gives of his father shows him as invariably kind and generous to wife and child, even if he did keep up the tradition of patriarchal authority. He is not recorded as making any opposition to Mistral's wish to devote his life to literature and 'Provence'. What will seem almost incredible in an age so essentially and universally (in spite of lip service) philistine and money-mad as ours, the old father had the most sincere respect, even reverence, for the poet's work. He whose reading was limited to the Bible, the *Imitatio* and Cervantes could not imagine the art of writing being misused for ignoble ends. He lived innocent of that 'popular' journalism, in all its forms whether book or periodical, which is the exploiter's hired assassin, and real literature's worst enemy. At times when Frédéric was at home and work pressed, Maître François would call out sharply for him to come and do his share of work. But if the young mother replied that he was writing, a softened voice instantly replied: "Then don't disturb him!"

The death of his father made a sharp break in Mistral's life. In the division of property which followed, the Mas dóu Juge did not fall to his lot; and for a man of his temperament the loss of his old home was painful, following so immediately on the greater grief for his father. He suffered, too, at the sight of all the familiar household goods brought out in front of the Mas and divided by an expert into three separate lots for the heirs. Among Mistral's share was a house in the village of Maillane, called the House of the Lizard, which still stands, just opposite the house which he built for himself and his wife when they married in 1876. The last pang of separation from the old life came when he and his mother were carried slowly away from the Mas in the farm wagon which also bore the household goods they had inherited. Henceforth Mistral's life was the enviable one of a successful man of letters whose private income allowed him to write and to publish only what and when he pleased.

Naturally, the seven years during which *Mirèio* was composed were not wholly occupied by even so absorbing a task. The account of some of his amusements and expeditions with friends may be read in *Moun Espelido*, but there are one or two literary events of a collective kind which must be recorded if only because of their relation to the Félibres and the revival of the *langue d'oc* as the language of poetry. And here is the moment to speak of the importance of Roumanille as a predecessor of Mistral. One may legitimately question Mariéton's too unqualified statement about Roumanille as poet—in comparison, that is to say, with Jasmin and Gélu. Good as Roumanille is as poet—and the anthology piece *Mounte Vole Mouri*, however over-quoted, is evidence of his powers, quite apart from his other poems—he is even more notable as organiser and above all as language expert. Clearly, when you have a group of gifted young men, it is impossible to allot exactly to each his share in a collective achievement. Mistral was the 'divine' poet of the set, and that they all acknowledged with a pleasant disregard for self. But the older man, Roumanille, had his importance too.

The anthology of contemporary poets of the *langue d'oc* collected by Roumanille, and published in 1852 at Avignon under the title *Li Prouvençalo*, was not the most essential service he performed. Of course, to a group of young writers, impatient to be known and full of illusions about the public response to poets, the publication of the anthology must have seemed Roumanille's greatest achievement. But most of the contributors were not very important, although the publication revealed Mistral, Aubanel and Mathieu as well as Roumanille himself; and to us perhaps the most striking piece of 'news' about it is that the critical sponsor was that Professor Saint-René Taillandier who, through no fault of his own, had earlier covered himself with glory by awarding an unknown Mistral his Baccalauréat. Although Mistral at the time when this anthology was published had barely reached the age of twenty-two, Saint-René Taillandier in his preface spoke of him as "the counsellor, the censor, the severe but sympathetic judge" of the attempts then being made to establish a canon of Provençal.

Though the *Tresor dóu Felibrige* was the work of Mistral, the part played by Roumanille in these early days should always be fairly acknowledged. It was Roumanille who from the first insisted on the difficult but essential enterprise of trying to re form what one might call a "classical *langue d'oc*" from the many local dialects into which the language had been split by what Sainte-Beuve called its "misfortunes". True, any one of these local dialects was *understood* from Barcelona to Nice, and in a large area from the Loire to the seas, and similarly a person familiar with one of the dialects could understand the others, but this was far indeed from constituting a literary language worthy of serious intellectual and poetic thinking. There was not even agreement on some little points of grammar, still less was there any agreed convention of spelling. And, as always, purely individual phonetic spelling resulted in something like chaos. Making all allowances for differences of time and place, the situation was not unlike that in Italy in the early days when each poet wrote in the dialect of his native city, and no Dante had arisen to fix the primacy of Tuscany. For the *langue d'oc* of 1852 there was the added complication that in "French of Paris" the area already possessed a mature and beautiful classical language. Why want another? "Because it is ours!" they might have answered, "Because it carries the traditions of our people." The notion that the *langue d'oc* (Provençal) is simply French debased and mispronounced by the uncultured Midi is so strongly rooted a prejudice that at the risk of being tiresome I must insist that Provençal and French are as much independent languages sprung from popular Latin as Portuguese and Spanish. The great colonising achievements of the Portuguese have carried their language to old and new nations across the world, but so far as Europe is concerned more people still speak Provençal than speak Portuguese.

The problem was complex—what was to be taken as the standard language, who was to determine it, and how were the writers to be persuaded to accept it? With his usual energy and public spirit, his love of groups, Roumanille organised congresses of poets—at Arles in 1852, and at Aix-en-Provence in 1853. The first of these had at least the merit of introducing to each other many writers of the *langue d'oc* who had never before met. The second produced another anthology, *Lou Roumavàgi dei Troubaires*—the Troubadours' Festival, for from the beginning the group liked to stress the idea that poetry is social and festive and popular, not the mysterious vaticination of grimly superior solitaries. But so far as composing their linguistic differences was concerned, they achieved nothing. The poets of other areas were in no hurry to submit to the standards proposed by this youthful Avignon group, whose growing popularity perhaps made the others a little jealous. Jasmin and Gélu were particularly contemptuous. Jasmin, with all his poetic gifts, was rather like a modern *prêtre ouvrier* in his disdain for the festive and sociable side of what was to be the Félibrige, could detect no 'uplift' in poetry recitals and eloquent discourses preceded by *aiòli* and a generous Côtes du

Rhône vintage. Gélu, with his bitter class hatred and acrimonious pauperism, was even more violent and hostile. The noble and enthusiastic preface which Mistral wrote in 1886 for the complete works of Gélu was the gesture of a gentleman and an honest critic who would not allow past differences to prejudice judgment. But in the 1850s Mistral had to admit that the 'congresses' had failed in their main objective. As he himself wrote later, there was no sign of an agreement for a reform of the *langue d'oc,* and the proposals of the Avignonnais were disdained. And there was surely some reason as well as prejudice in the rejection, above all since the unifying and dominant genius of Mistral had not been revealed. The Avignonnais wanted to take as a standard the speech of the lower Rhône area—their own! But historically hardly any of the great troubadours of the Moyen Age had come from Provence, and the two best living poets preferred their own dialects—Agen and Marseille. So did the smaller men. And who can blame them? A 'movement' so essentially based on local patriotism was bound to meet the patriotic resistance of still smaller areas.

A way out of this impasse was found at the now celebrated banquet of May 21st, 1854, at Font-Ségugne, when the society of the Félibres was founded and they decided to start the *Armana Prouvençau,* which has continued to appear annually until the present time. Since it was impossible to secure agreement among all the poets of the *langue d'oc,* well, seven poets of the Avignon area would make a fraternal agreement, and hope that in time the quality of their creative work, their labours to build a living and dignified poetic language from the dialects, and their popular Almanac would in time persuade the others to come in.

Font-Ségugne is the name of a property close to the village of Châteauneuf-de-Gadagne (about seven miles from Avignon on Route Nationale 100), which belonged to the Giéra family, one of whom, Paul, was a poet as well as notary. The estate belonged before the Revolution to an aristocratic family, the Dukes of Gadagne, from whom it passed to a certain Monsieur

Goujon. He, for reasons unexplained, bequeathed it together with a considerable fortune to a grocer of Avignon, Baptiste Giéra, from whom it passed to his sons, Paul and Jules. By the way, it is characteristic of Mistral's passion for his language that in his account of this historic little banquet he is careful to derive the name from *font*, a spring, and *seguido*, continual, which flows near the little château! The Giéras were hospitable and in easy circumstances, so that they often acted as hosts to the poets and the "*quauqui damisello graciouso*" (pretty girls) who accompanied them. On May 21st, 1854, the poets present were:

Paul Giéra (1816–1861)
Joseph Roumanille (1818–1891)
Frédéric Mistral (1830–1914)
Théodore Aubanel (1829–1886)
Anselme Mathieu (1828–1895)
Alphonse Tavan (1833–1905)
Jean Brunet (1823–1894)

It is a question how much, or rather how little, the readers I have in mind will care to know of these other poets grouped about Mistral and Roumanille. Too many unfamiliar names and writings may discourage a reader's good-will, while to pass them over without further comment as mere 'attendant lords' looks lazy and may disappoint legitimate curiosity. The main points to keep in mind about this founding of the Félibrige are, I think, these: it was never intended to be an exclusive clique, but a nucleus to which other poets in numbers would be welcomed; it was not promulgating a poetic doctrine outside of which was no literary salvation; it aimed at maintaining or reviving the historic and traditional life of Provence and the dignity of the *langue d'oc*, within which limits the poets were free to write as they chose. Indeed the close association of Alphonse Daudet with the Félibrige shows an even wider tolerance, since he wrote in French and in his various Tartarins satirised the Provençaux.

Aubanel, according to the received opinion, was the most

gifted of these poets after Mistral. He fell in love with one of the *damisello graciouso*, Jenny Manivet, whom he met and courted at Font-Ségugne, but . . It is a pathetic little tragedy, but for some reason Jenny abandoned lover, family, and the cheerful society of the Félibres to become a nun. It is said that she was sent by her Superior to Constantinople, where she died in the same year as Aubanel without ever having seen him. What motives and emotions underlay this renunciation are not explained, but the poet has recorded his passion and his grief in his best-known book, the *Mióugrano entreduberto*—the Cleft Pomegranate, emblem of a broken heart. A later book of erotic poems, *Li Fiho d'Avignoun* (The Girls of Avignon), though privately printed, caused the ageing poet much trouble owing to the censorious godly—a mishap which is said to have hastened his death. Is it worth recording that Aubanel's play, *Lou Pan dóu Pecat* (The Bread of Sin), was one of the very few works of the Félibres which were acceptable to the critic, Arthur Symons.

The others are less important. Anselme Mathieu, a fantasist and amorist, was dear to Mistral as a person, if we may judge from the tenderness with which he is treated in *Moun Espelido*. His poems are trifles light as air, but full of charm and grace. At the Centenary a pilgrimage was made to his birthplace at Châteauneuf-du-Pape. Sad to relate, in his later years he lost his money and was forced to turn innkeeper, and as his clients were mainly poets he "did not make a fortune". As a poet Brunet hardly exists, and his main difficulty seems to have been to make a living. He worked as a glazier, a decorative painter, a musician, a fireman and a dealer in antiques, dying so poor that he was buried at the expense of his native town, Avignon. His great work, which he left unfinished, was a collection of 14,000 Provençal proverbs. Who would have thought there were so many in the world?

Tavan, last but not least of the seven, represents one of the pleasant aspects of the Félibrige—its welcome without condescension or patronage of any poet however humble his condition. Here we see the humanity of Roumanille and

63

Mistral, their sense of the true values, a fraternity of talent which the Félibres have wisely preserved. At the Centenary banquet it was very pleasant to me to see peasants and small employees and *gardians* on terms of perfect ease and fraternity with Monsieur Daladier and the suffragan Bishop of Avignon and Frédéric Mistral *neveu*. Tavan, like Charloun, was a poor land labourer, who had to leave school at the age of twelve to start work. His best-known work is the gay song *Li Frisoun de Marieto* (Mariette's Curls) and his most touching the poems on the death of his wife and, four years later, his daughter. His vocation for poetry was revealed to him by reading the Psalms. He served as a private in the French garrison in Rome, where he contracted malaria, and this left him too weak to work on the land, until his friends found him employment on the old P.L.M. Railway. He outlived all the original seven except Mistral, and was honoured along with the greater poet in May 1904, the fiftieth anniversary.

Such were the seven founders of the Félibrige. Mistral's belief in the mystical significance of the number 'seven' was again in evidence here. If the three sevens in the date, May 21st, were a mere coincidence, that could hardly be the case with the seven poets. If we look at them we see at once that three (Mistral, Roumanille and Aubanel) were the real brains and centre of the new group. Three were little better than supernumerary actors, and the seventh (Mathieu) was so much a fantasist that even Mistral, who rejoiced exceedingly in his friend's caprices, can scarcely have expected much, if any, serious work from him. It seems likely that Mistral had talked over the situation beforehand with Roumanille and Aubanel, and that the other four were brought in for the official opening ceremony as a stage army and to make up the mystic seven. What is amazing is that the Félibrige, with such a modest and private beginning, should have exerted so wide an influence and have lasted so long.

The nineteenth century (which lasted until 1914) was fertile in poetic 'schools', particularly in Paris. After the Romantiques came the Parnassiens, and then the Décadents (admirably satirised in the *Déliquescences d'Adoré Floupette*), the Symbolistes, followed by such an outbreak of 'schools' that a new one with its attendant magazine was founded practically every publishing season. Obviously the best of these 'schools' made contributions to French literature—even the Décadents, if we count Paul Verlaine among them—but they are now all a matter of history. Nobody now calls himself a Parnassien or a Symboliste, and I doubt if even Jules Romains (de l'Académie Française!) would care to be reminded that he was once an ardent Unanimiste, indeed the only Unanimiste. Only the Félibres have outlasted the century, and are far more numerous and more influential than when they started, though even they would not claim that the *langue d'oc* today possesses a poet equal to Mistral.

The explanation lies in the names themselves. The French 'schools' chose, or had chosen for them, names or nicknames which were supposed to indicate a poetic programme, a literary doctrine. Once that doctrine had been worked out, the programme achieved, the impulse behind the names vanished and they became simply tags for literary historians. The Félibrige escaped this fate although it certainly had a programme and a doctrine, chiefly because its aims were much higher and less self-centred than those of the ordinary literary 'school', and partly because the vagueness of the names 'Félibres' and 'Félibrige' meant that they were adequate to cover the activities of succeeding generations. In its widest sense 'Félibrige' simply means the cult of Provence and Provençal speech, and ought to last as long as they do; in its narrowest sense it is still wide enough to include all who follow Mistral and are inspired by his example and ideas. Victor Hugo (*hélas!*) may be the greatest French poet—I don't say "of France" because Mistral is "of France" just as much—but he certainly has not had so continuous and happy an influence.

The word 'Félibres' was certainly Mistral's discovery and it was adopted on his suggestion. Already in that we can see his gift for organisation and popularity—I don't care to say 'propaganda' since both word and thing have become so

65

degraded. What does 'Félibres' mean? Really not much more in the *langue d'oc* than in French or English. Mistral found it in an ancient Provençal poem on the traditional theme of the seven griefs or agonies of the Virgin. The fourth was when the youthful Jesus was lost for three days, and the Virgin tells him how they found him in the Temple:

> "Que vous disputavias
> Emé li tiroun de la Lèi,
> Emé li sèt felibre de la Lèi . . ."

He was disputing with the doctors of the Law, with the seven *félibres* of the Law. There has been even more dispute about the origin and meaning of the word. According to Maître Julian, some have derived it from a Low Latin *felibris*, meaning a babe or suckling; others from a Greek *philebraios* (which I don't find in Liddell and Scott) said to mean a lover of Hebrew and a lover of the beautiful. A Teutonic origin has been suggested, and somebody (possibly Bonaparte Wyse) suggested that it was Irish. Mistral gives his views in the *Trésor*, and somebody put out the ingenious suggestion that the word was a popular corruption of the Hebrew *sephem* de la Lèi. Finally the whole question was reviewed by a philologist in the learned review, *Romania*, and he came to the conclusion that *'félibre'* derived from the Spanish *feligres*, meaning a parishioner or follower, itself derived from *filius ecclesiæ* which in medieval Latin (it is said) can mean one of the faithful or even a priest. In modern Catalan it means a choir-boy. As a descriptive title for a poetic doctrine it is obviously meaningless. But what excellent publicity all this discussion was! Human minds, particularly the minds of students and scholars in literary matters, delight in endless discussion of problems, especially linguistic problems, of little or no importance. The habit is not confined to France —the correspondence columns of the London Sunday journals used to exhibit astonishing examples of triviality and the futility of semi-learned wrangling. At twenty-three Mistral could scarcely have realised this fact, so all this extraneous advertising of the name must be put down to a lucky accident which made him pick on a name which had the advantage (for him) of being connected with the *seven* griefs of the Virgin Mother. But he is surely entitled to praise for his wisdom and skill in selecting a word which gave no handle to enemies, meant practically nothing, and could be made to mean almost anything the Félibres chose. What they chose above all to make it mean was the cult and expression of Provençal life and traditions.

According to Mistral's recollections, confirmed by others, this 'historic' feast at Font-Ségugne was the occasion for two other decisions of importance to Mistral and the whole Félibrige movement. When Mistral had quoted to his friends the line about "the seven *félibres* of the Law", Giéra asked, "But what is the law?" And Mistral instantly gave the promise that he would compile the 'Law' of the Félibres, by which he did not mean the organisation under a *capoulié* which was made public in 1876 but the immense labour of his encyclopædia-dictionary *Lou Tresor dóu Felibrige*. Twenty-three is an ideal age for making grandiose plans. Mistral has the distinction of having carried out his, though even he could scarcely have foreseen the work he would have to put into it before the two large volumes at last appeared in 1886. A foreigner who is no philologist can offer no valid opinion on such a work, which had a wider and more picturesque scope than Dr. Johnson's dictionary, and must have needed greater industry and a greater practical knowledge. The *Trésor* was not taken solely from books, but from personal knowledge of the 'folk' who used the still living tongue. Of course Mistral had many helpers, but then so had Johnson, though Mistral had the priceless advantage of not being forced to labour at the task for his bread.

A friend has given us a glimpse of Mistral's energy and scruple in collecting technical words. They were together in a fishing boat at sea. Mistral, from his life-long experience of the Rhône and its boat traffic, knew the river terms for sails and rigging and fishing-nets and so forth. The friend watched Mistral as he talked with the sailors. He would touch some part of the boat or its equipment and say: "Where I come from we call this so-and-so. What do you call it?" and would carefully note the reply. Perhaps, as some complain, he was a little too optimistically ready to find survivals of ancient Greek words in the vocabulary of the fishermen. The words he quotes certainly look Greek, but then it seems improbable that they could have survived for two thousand years amid all the horrors and violence and destruction of incessant wars and barbarian invasions. More plausibly they might have come from Byzantium during the Crusades or later by way of Italian. Few poets have known their language as thoroughly as Mistral knew his *langue d'oc*, and the influence of his studies as a lexicographer may be traced in the notes to his poems and has survived among the Félibres, who are often very much alive to the hidden meaning of place and other names. It may seem strange, as Emile Léonard remarks, to speak of the 'erudition' of a popular poet, but it is a fact.

The other decision made at Font-Ségugne was to launch the Almanac, the *Armana Provençau*, which still continues to appear. It was essentially an appeal to the people, as the *Trésor* was essentially a service to the writers. The title added to its frankly popular appeal, and Mistral's acknowledged weakness for the prognostications of Nostradamus may suggest to the English reader a Provençal version of Old Moore's Almanac. In point of fact it was and is far less crude, and much more a true miscellany of poetry and prose, of popular traditions and aspirations as well as the mirth of poets. A complete set of the Almanac has the double disadvantage of being bulky and expensive, and even odd numbers are hard to find. Probably the most practical way to learn a little about the best side of the *Armana* is through the three volumes of Mistral's prose collected from it, and from the prose writings of Roumanille— if the latter ever come back into print. Mistral has other claims on our regard, but in these prose pieces Roumanille is seen at his best. According to Mistral, the circulation of the Almanac in the first year (1855) amounted to only 500 copies, but gradually rose, and by the end of the century, in spite of the set-back of the Franco-Prussian War, it reached 10,000. The total audience must have been very much larger. Not all those who spoke the *langue d'oc* were able to read, and it has been noted that people who are entirely without knowledge of letters are usually more responsive to poetry and the poetic view of life than those who possess that smattering of knowledge which leaves them so open to the vulgar corruption of the baser type of periodical. Copies of the Almanac were handed round the villages, read aloud on winter nights to little groups in cottages and lonely farm-houses. The *Armana Prouvençau* was not exclusively 'popular'. It contained many pieces which might be thought more or less 'highbrow'. But its merit is the purity of its intentions. It did not try to exploit or intimidate or degrade the people for interested motives, but to instruct by amusing them, to kindle in them that love of Provence which was the motive of the Félibrige.

4

'Mirèio'

Not long after the death of his father, when Mistral had moved with his mother to the House of the Lizard in Maillane, he wrote and had engraved three lines of verse—some say on a sun-dial, some on the lintel of the door. They seem more appropriate to a sun-dial than to a doorway, but it doesn't matter. What matters is the sentiment:

> Bèu lesert, béu toun soulèu,
> L'ouro passo que trop lèu,
> E, deman, ploura, belèu.

(Beautiful lizard, drink the sunlight, Time speeds only too fast, Tomorrow perhaps it will rain.)*

Obviously, nobody is going to suggest that what a poet puts on his sun-dial is to be taken as serious evidence for or against his character. But this Provençal version of *carpe diem* may suggest a hint to any student of Mistral who is liable to make the poet too much the earnest man-of-letters. It is natural enough when you read of his great dictionary, of long carefully-wrought narrative poems and all the other activities. Mistral was far too good an artist not to know that good work in art means hard work for the artist, for only the amateur imagines that it can all be done on 'inspiration'. Of course Mistral worked, and no doubt in the *"ohne Hast, ohne Rast"* way praised by Goethe; but he certainly didn't smash his eggs, shell and all, to make his omelette. Like the Lizard of his lintel, or sun-dial, he could and did enjoy the passing hour for what it brings, apart from any thought of gain or self-improvement.

* There are three rather similar lines in *Mirèio*.

He was as ready for 'a frisk' as Dr. Johnson, and far less clumsily. His warm-hearted, sociable nature always responded to the calls of friendship and innocent pleasure. As examples I would point to the expedition with some of his bachelor Félibre friends to Mont Ventoux—which ended in their being arrested as vagabonds—and the even more delightful story of how they ate eel-stew in one of the last surviving eating places of the Rhône boatmen in Arles, an expedition which Alphonse Daudet has described.

A friendly, not to say convivial, temperament like this naturally made Mistral many friends, but at the same time he evidently had a great deal of what is called 'tact'. Even if we had no evidence for it, a moment's reflection would show that this 'tact' must have existed to hold together his miscellaneous team of poets and southerners among whom claims and susceptibilities ran high. *Tartarin de Tarascon* is a parody, but it does bring out the ineradicable Southern habit of 'imagining things' from a very slight or no basis at all. Even Mistral with all his geniality and tact could not wholly avoid such disagreeable incidents as the quarrels about his Arles statue and the library which went to Avignon and the quarrels among his followers, including the now too famous differences between Roumanille and Aubanel.

One of the pleasant traits in Mistral is that he didn't mind making fun of himself. It is only an inference, but I think justified, that he included in his memoirs his satirical story of the tactful mayor in order to poke fun at himself. It appeared in the *Armana Prouvençau* in 1883, nearly thirty years after the time we are considering, and it is told of an alleged schoolfellow who for decades had been mayor of Gigognan—fifty years, in fact, during which time there had been eleven governments, not one of which had dismissed this Provençal secular Vicar of Bray. How was it done? Mistral asks. And the mayor takes him round the town to show him. They come on some players at *boules*, and the mayor has a compliment for someone's skill. They pass two girls, and the mayor remarks to Mistral in a sufficiently loud aside: "What pretty little faces!" They meet a

71

local wrestler whose age has forced retirement—the mayor reminds him of old triumphs. Then it is the curé, and the mayor feels the church is too small for the congregation . . . perhaps a government grant may be had. Farther on, the mayor reprimands a lad who had fought with a rival, but in such a way that it is as much a compliment as a warning to keep the peace. "I see," says Mistral, "you use soft soap!" At that moment they get into conversation with an old woman with whom the mayor jokes. At last she turns to Mistral and says: "You see, he knows everyone and talks to us all, down to the smallest child. So he's been mayor for fifty years and will be as long as he lives!"

Such amiable traits and tactics no doubt go a long way towards explaining Mistral's influence and popularity in his own district, but they do not account for the great and immediate success of *Mirèio* in Paris. It is perhaps too pessimistic to say that no genuine work of permanent value is ever immediately successful without some lucky accident of influence and patronage. Yet, in spite of the applause of the Félibres, would *Mirèio* have succeeded as it did without the aid of Adolphe Dumas and of Lamartine? And the enthusiastic aid of Adolphe Dumas—if we may believe the story as told— was itself due to a series of lucky chances.

There is said to be no interest now in the writings of Adolphe Dumas—I have not read them—but in the 1850s he enjoyed the favour of a large reading public. He was, as his name implies, a native of Provence, and a friend of the Imperial Minister for Education, who came from Digne. He it was who entrusted Dumas with the official mission of going round Provence to collect the traditional folk songs. Though Dumas had acquired the usual prejudices in favour of Paris, he was genuinely a child of the people, and owed his education to a strangely romantic chance. He had a very pretty elder sister, who ran away with a troop of strolling actors, and soon found herself destitute and crying in the streets of Paris. A wealthy man, passing in his carriage, was struck with her beauty and grief, questioned her, recognised that her story was true and that she was honest, educated, and finally married her. In due course she sent for her young brother and educated him, and he as a young man was caught up in the Romantic literary movement of 1830.

Here was a set of curious accidents needed to bring Adolphe Dumas back to Provence as a well-known writer seeking folk songs on behalf of the Ministry of Education! Once he was back in Provence on that errand he could hardly help learning of so popular a person as young Frédéric Mistral, and in due course knocked on the door of the 'Lizard's House' in Maillane. When the visitor enquired about folk songs Mistral sang him the dawn song of *Magali* from *Mireille*, with its hauntingly beautiful opening:

> O Magali, ma tant amado,
> Mete la tèsto au fenestroun!
> Escouto un pau aquesto aubado
> De tambourin e de vióuloun.
> Es plen d'estello, aperamount!
> L'auro es toumbado,
> Mai lis estello paliran,
> Quand te veiran!

The theme is most ancient, as old as dynastic Egypt, the 'lovers' metamorphosis'—the girl protesting that she will change herself into fish or bird or grass or cloud to avoid the importunate lover and he finding always an imagined metamorphosis to win her. At last she protests she will die to evade him—and he will be the earth to take her to his heart. Of course it was folk, and it wasn't folk. Mistral had taken the old song, as Burns took those of his own country, and improved it by re-writing. It is the kind of poem which every highbrow despises, and ten million people after a century still sing. The choice no doubt was an obvious one, but then it was first necessary to write the poem. In any event Adolphe Dumas was enchanted: "Where the devil did you find that?"

Mistral explained that it came from a long poem he was writing in Provençal, and, after listening patiently to the usual

73   F

patronising diatribe on the absurdity of writing in *patois*, read Dumas some stanzas of *Mirèio*. Mistral could not afterwards remember which stanzas they were, but Dumas expressed his admiration, though after he had begun by speaking of modern Provençal as a *patois* and "a language in rags" it seems a little unlikely that he should instantly have been converted to the point of view of the Félibres and have made the discourse attributed to him. But at any rate Mistral had made a friend, to himself, his poem and his programme.

This was demonstrated some three years later, in 1859, when having finished but not yet published his poem Mistral took the manuscript copy to Paris. He called on Adolphe Dumas and, at his request, read him the whole poem in three long sittings. Then was seen the advantage—if it was an advantage —of friendly relations with a journalist. The student and indeed the practitioner of literary strategy should meditate the puff which Adolphe Dumas sent to the *Gazette de France* in Paris:

"The *Gazette du Midi* has already informed the *Gazette de France* that Frédéric Mistral is here. Who is Frédéric Mistral? Nobody seems to know. I am asked the question, and I am afraid of putting my reply in words which will not be believed, they are so unexpected, and come at a time when the vogue of imitative poetry seems to prove only the death of poetry and of poets.

"In ten years the Académie Française will accept yet another great literary work, long after everyone else. The Institut's clock is often an hour late in the centuries. I want to be the first to reveal what might be called to-day the Virgil of Provence, the Mantuan shepherd arriving in Rome with poetry worthy of Gallus and Scipio.

"Our fair land of the South, which is twice Roman— Roman Latin and Roman Catholic—has so often longed for a poem in its immortal language which would enshrine its sacred beliefs and high morality. I have the poem in my hands, a poem of twelve cantos. It is the work of Frédéric

74

Mistral of the village of Maillane and signed with his name. I countersign it on my word of honour which I have never betrayed, and on my full responsibility which asks for nothing but justice."

This now seems rather crude propaganda, and, in fact, several newspapers made fun of it. But Dumas evidently knew his public and was pleased with the effect made, though Mistral does not seem to have been so happy about it. At all events Dumas made up for any slight annoyance caused by introducing Mistral to Lamartine the very next day. This was a valuable service, for Lamartine in addition to his great literary reputation had been a member of the Provisional Government during the Revolution of 1848. He had not been very successful as a ruler, but his prestige and amazing gifts as a popular orator had averted some of the disorders and excesses inevitable in a working-class revolt staged by politicians. Unlike Hugo, he had not quarrelled with Louis Napoleon or vowed a furious vendetta of outraged vanity like the author of *Les Châtiments*. Unfortunately the expenses of his brief tenure of office had left Lamartine heavily in debt—a proof of the honest and disinterested service he had given—and in 1859 he was still slaving at histories and biographies to keep alive, and it was not until some time later that the Imperial Government gave him a pension of 20,000 gold francs. Among other works at this time he was bringing out a series of essays (or *entretiens* as he called them) on literary subjects under the general title of *Cours familier de Littérature*. He had been brought up in the country near Macon, where the language spoken by the peasants was still closely allied to Provençal, and Lamartine had talked it almost exclusively until he was twelve; so that he had no difficulty in understanding Mistral's verse.

Both Mistral and Lamartine have left accounts of this first interview. According to a letter written to Roumanille almost immediately afterwards, Mistral heard that he had been praised to Lamartine independently by Dumas and another friend, Reboul; and from them Lamartine had heard of the three (then young) Provençal poets—Roumanille the dramatic, Aubanel the lyric, and Mistral the epic. They then talked of Arles, the Crau, the Camargue, country which Lamartine knew well; and at his request Mistral recited the opening stanzas of *Mirèio*. "He was delighted and thought it softer even than Italian." The ladies of Lamartine's family then came in, and the poet repeated his verses with great applause from them. On leaving Lamartine urged him to print his poem on fine paper, and added: "Send me a copy and I'll write to you."

Lamartine's account, written later, after the publication of the poem, is less accurate and contains some quite imaginary details, such as the *"beau and modeste jeune homme"* arriving in the sunset to dine—whereas in fact Mistral had been told to call after dinner. Nothing is said about the interest shown by the ladies. He thought Mistral had recited a lyric ("which pleased without enchanting"), a form "too narrow for his genius which needed the wide scope of the epic."

The use of the word 'epic' to describe *Mirèio* seems a mistake, especially since Mistral himself modestly calls it merely a "Provençal poem", which is exactly what it is. At the time Lamartine had great prestige and naturally what he wrote was taken up and echoed by the smaller writers, so that, in spite of his own disclaimer by silence, Mistral was labelled the 'epic poet' that critics feel they must discuss. Arthur Symons, for instance, spends some pains to point out—quite justly in my opinion—that Mistral was not an epic poet in the sense that Homer and Dante are. Symons was so much the decadent-about-town that one is a little surprised to find him interested by work so homely, rustic and traditional. But the æsthete and critic in Symons in their own way were as genuine as the poet, and he was always ready to recognise good work even when it was so different in every respect from his own tastes; and he did not wait for the Nobel Prize to discover Mistral. Symons's approach was more open-minded and appreciative than that of the Parisian Goncourt, who saw in Mistral only a peasant whose constant public speaking had developed his throat in the vulgar way often seen in singers at café concerts!

Although these distant literary comparisons are not really of much help in appreciating a modern poet, it is perhaps worth recording that Symons goes on to suggest Theocritus as the true classical inspirer of Mistral. This seems indisputable if we limit it to episodes such as, e.g., the gathering of mulberry leaves for the silk-worms with the refrain, *"Cantas, cantas, magnarello"*, and the description of the flock of sheep *en transhumance*, and the shepherd who tries to give Mireille a wooden cup he has carved during the long solitary watchful hours. *Magnarelles* was the name given to the girls whose duties included the care of the caterpillars and spinning of the silk cocoons; and the Museon Arlaten has specimens of carving by shepherds of remarkable designs, some traditional and others suggested by Nature. Among them is at least one cup such as Mistral describes, so the Theocritean likeness is not all literary copying but the result of a similar culture and its art expression at a distance of more than two thousand years.

If, on the other hand, we consider the story of the poem as a whole, the likeness is not to Theocritus but to the late Greek novelists, especially the *Daphnis and Chloe* of Longus, without their absurdities, coincidences and conventional endings. *Mirèio* is a Provençal *Daphnis and Chloe* of a much more wholesome and authentic rusticity, a tale of two young lovers told with delicate restraint and modesty, an idyll which for all their mutual devotion and trust in the Saintes Maries ended tragically—the blithe sensuality of the Greek tale is lost in the more ideal sentiment of Catholicism. There is another difference. With Longus the country scenes and characters are obviously 'literary', and the descriptions seem paraphrased from Theocritus or suggest transcripts from lost pastoral poets. With Mistral there is hardly a trace of 'literary' influence in such scenes, which make up so large a part of the poem. All is authentic Provençal tradition learned at first hand from living witness, personal observation, and an imagination which keeps within the area of Provençal experience. True, the scenes at the sorcerer's cave and the apparitions of the Saintes Maries are outside ordinary human experience, but they are entirely within the imaginative experience of Mistral's characters. For all its grace and charm and poetic language there is something factitious about *Daphnis and Chloe*, a very select bucolic setting for a love tale for wealthy city dwellers. In comparison Mistral's idyll and its setting are almost realistic.

I say 'almost' because though Mistral's characters, ambience, descriptions and traditional life are as essentially authentic as those of Longus are 'literary', still we have to admit a certain idealisation in Mistral's handling.

This idyll of the loves of Vincent, the son of the poor wandering basket-weaver, and of Mireille, the daughter of the rich *ménager*, ending with Mireille's tragic death at the Saintes Maries, is the framework, the 'story', in which Mistral has managed to include so much of 'Provence'. But Lamartine's 'Provence' is too extensive in the sense that *Mireille* is mostly limited to that part of Provence and Languedoc which Marie Mauron called "la Rouanesse", the shores and delta of the Rhône from Avignon to the Saintes Maries and the Mediterranean, 'Rhodanie'. The wealth of that area (including the independence of the Mistrals) came from the rich alluvial land between Avignon and Arles, but so much of the poetry and romantic legend came from the barren salt marshes of the Camargue with their cattlemen and horse-breeders, and the stony Crau with its nomadic shepherds. The owners of a herd of semi-wild cattle or of semi-wild Camargue horses or of a large flock of sheep were not poor; and Mistral has placed one of each among the suitors of Mireille, who might have been acceptable to the proud—one might say "purse-proud"—old father, Maître Ramon. But her heart is given to the poor man, the *vannier*, Vincent. The weaving of osiers and rushes is now mostly carried on by the gipsies, but Vincent and his father Ambroise are Provençaux. These *vanniers* were not vågabonds but skilled craftsmen, and some of their sensitive workmanship is preserved in that "ark of civilisation" the Museon Arlaten. Greed and folly have sacrificed this art to the shoddy factory products, though at any rate in Languedoc—and I think in Provence—there are still a few master-craftsmen producing

78

work which the machines can't equal. But the *vanniers* are poorer than ever, and those I see look sullenly angry. I don't wonder.

Before proceeding to a description of this most popular and attractive of Mistral's long poems I should like to glance at the use and abuse of the word 'folk-lore', which is defined rather extensively by the Oxford Dictionary as the beliefs, customs and legends of the common people. Who are the 'common people' and when do people cease to be 'common'? By what sign short of an Oxford degree shall we know them? In practice 'folk-lore' is a word generally limited to survivals from the pre-machine age, but as a matter of fact the machine-minders and their exploiters and parasites are as much given to "beliefs, customs and legends" as primitive agriculturists, with the difference that they are always lacking in poetry as well as any connection with the world of Nature. A belief in advertisements is not much of an advance on a belief in amulets, and the football pool is a poor substitute for the ancient mystery and dexterity of the *tauromachie*.

At any rate the word 'folk-lore' is now used as a term of reproach by critics, from which there is supposed to be no appeal. If an author (and presumably a painter or other artist) is guilty of 'folk-lore', then that's the end of him. It is used to discount D. H. Lawrence and his Hopi snake-dancers as well as Mistral and his Arlésiennes. The *galoubet* of Provence is as despised as the Indian hand-drum. And these superior-to-folk-lore persons shuffle about in awkward imitation of African voodoo prancings and melt at the cacophonous dronings of tin-pan alley! Still, it is from 'folk-lore' that we learn the complicated ritual of wooing in Provence, particularly the language of flowers, which is said to have been derived from the Arabs. Mistral in *Mirèio* neglects these for a more direct and less conventional approach, but he is true to Provençal folk-lore in the opposition of the parents to what they think undesirable suitors. Countess Martinengo-Cesaresco perhaps exaggerates, yet not greatly, when she says:

"The course of true love nowhere flows less smoothly than in old Provence. As soon as a country girl is suspected of having a liking for some youth, she is set upon by her family as if she were guilty of a monstrous crime. A microscopic distinction of rank, a divergence in politics, or a deficiency of money will be snatched at as the excuse for putting the lover under the ban of absolute proscription."

From which it naturally followed that the girl often eloped and, if a minor, in the presence of two witnesses to prove the girl's consent. Thus Mireille's parents put up an opposition to her marriage with Vincent which was rather the rule than the exception, something to be expected; and her running away differed from the ordinary elopement only in the fact that there were no witnesses, that she unwisely ran to the Saintes Maries instead of to Vincent, and that she died instead of being married by parents eager to make an honest woman of her.

Injustice is inevitably done a poem by summarising its plot, especially when it is no more than an idyll of disappointed love, with the obvious scenes of falling-in-love, rivalries of suitors, attempted murder of the hero by a rejected and jealous rival, opposition of parents, and the fatal ending. But from the beginning and throughout, the characters, the incidents, the descriptions of place and custom and morals form an incomparable and unforgettable series of pictures of the Provence of Mistral's youth, his own 'Rhodanie'. While the main merit of the poem—apart of course from the author's poetic genius—lies in this presentation of a people, so also does its difficulty for a foreigner, as the reader will no doubt have realised long ago. Mistral wrote his poem for the sake of preserving a still existing traditional way of life, but we must now pick up any remnants of that life for the sake of the poem. Mistral wrote for an audience who instantly took and appreciated every reference and allusion, while we as outsiders and late-comers have to pick up the knowledge as best we can—and of course it can't be acquired from footnotes however informative, but only from first-hand knowledge of the country as it still exists.

At the risk of seeming to insist on details let me point out one or two purely local allusions in the very first book, which describes the walk of Vincent and his father, and the evening at Maître Ramon's Mas. They have come from Vallabrégues (a Rhône-side hamlet north of Tarascon) going in the direction of the Crau. Towards sunset Vincent calls his father's attention to the heavy clouds gathering about the sun *"eila sus Magalouno"* —above Maguelone. Now of course from where the couple were they couldn't possibly see Maguelone, and to a stranger it is just a name, but Mistral wanted the name for its associations of the melancholy, the loneliness, the desolation and grandeur of that ruined city represented now only by a half-ruined Romanesque cathedral on a lonely sandbank of Bas-Languedoc.* You must see the place and know a little of its tragical history—twice destroyed, and each time by a King of France, the 'Franchiman' whose crimes against the Midi are not yet forgotten! The lines are not indeed so inevitable and thrilling as Dante's, but for those who can and will allow their imagination to follow as Mistral intended there is something of the magic of:

"Era già l'ora che volge il disio
ai naviganti, e intenerisce il cuore . . ."

in the simpler words of Vincent:

"Paire, diguè Vincèn, espinchas lou soulèu!
Vesès, eila sus Magalouno,
Coume lou nivo l'empielouno!"

Then again, the mere name of Maître Ramon's farm, the Mas di Falabrego, which means nothing to a stranger, has a meaning for those who understand it and who love fine trees. The *falabrego* is the *micocoulier*, the *Celtis Australis* of the botanists, which for some reason not clear to me we call the nettle-tree. It is a smooth-barked, tall, imposing tree, something between a beech and a walnut, and characteristic of the Midi and of the

* There is a famous legend of 'Pierre de Provence et la belle Maguelonne'.

81

Mas, where it is planted for shade. I daresay we might find that, as is the case with other trees, some of the finest specimens of the nettle-tree are in Kew Gardens, but I never saw one outside of Provence-Languedoc. There are some lovely ones in the ancient Botanical Garden of Montpellier. Children still like the yellow berries which in Mistral's time formed part of the frugal yet varied diet of the people. Do not be misled by the similarity of the name Fabrégues, a village near Montpellier. There are no *micocouliers*, and the word means a forge or smithy.

More of the past, unfortunately, is Maître Ambroise's description of the rows of splendid olive trees—as many rows as there are days in the year and as many trees in each row—with some strips of vine and almond. Propaganda and heaven knows what misguided though doubtless well-meaning economic policy have tended to substitute the cultivation of inferior wines for the production of excellent olive-oil. The olive-oil of Salon is still highly esteemed. "What a lot of olive-pickers there must be," says Vincent naïvely. And his father explains, what Vincent must have known, that in the late autumn the girls of the neighbourhood come as volunteers for olive-picking, and make work a holiday fête—just as the *gardians* of the Camargue help each *manade* in turn in branding the cattle and make the *ferrade* a festival instead of a dull paid task.

These allusions are all contained in fewer than thirty lines of the first book of *Mirèio*, and they ought to indicate what Lamartine meant when he said that the theme of the poem is Provence. Page after page might be filled with similar illustrations from the first book alone. There are two others which must at least be mentioned. After the two basket-makers have reached the farm and started work, supper is served on the stone table outside, under the trees, for coolness' sake. Though this is a well-off farmer, who owns a flock of sheep as well as arable land needing six ploughs, the olives, the vines and almonds, the silk-raising and bee-keeping, he eats with his men a frugal meal of bread and wine and beans. In

82

accordance with ancient custom, the women eat apart; and Mireille, though the only daughter, waits on the farm servants, who, again according to old custom, each in turn give an account of their day's work, until Mistral abruptly breaks in on his narrative with the cry of grief and regret for lost days:

"Coume au mas, coume au tèms de moun paire, ai! ai ai!" (As they did at the Mas, in my father's time, alas! alas!) Pedants have objected to this on the grounds that the sudden touch of personal emotion is an intrusion which "spoils the illusion". But why create an illusion? Mistral's object here was not illusion but reality made poetic.

The other allusion is a matter of general history which seems to have been largely forgotten outside France. After the supper Maître Ambroise sings a ballad about the defeat of the English ships by Admiral Suffren. Anyone who looks up naval history will see how near Suffren came to wresting from the British Navy its supremacy in the Indian Ocean. He was one of the great French admirals, and thousands of tourists pass his statue on the quay at St. Tropez without, apparently, knowing who he was or having the curiosity to enquire. He is as genuine a 'hero' of Provence as the alleged Provençal killer of Nelson is an invention.

Thus, at the very beginning of Mistral's first long poem, we see how he brought together the sites, customs, traditions, characters, legends and superstitions of Provence. Naturally, a brief exposition based on the opening pages of the poem must be superficial and limited as well as defective; there has, for instance, been no account taken of the belief in sorcery which occupies so much of the sixth book or of the deep faith in religious legends which is the main theme of the last three.

The part played by legends in the life of the Oxford Dictionary's 'common people' in Provence was very considerable, particularly in the settled agricultural epoch. A similar or greater credulity exists among the industrialised 'common people', but their 'legends' are political, social and economic, are often deliberately and cynically invented by propaganda and advertising, and are totally without poetry or moral and religious meaning. The credulity of the agricultural epoch was on the whole creative; that of the industrial epoch is mainly destructive. A genuine legend is never based on the self-created falsehoods of its subject. A saint does not plant out embellished stories of himself to persuade people that he is holy and has performed miracles. The faith and imagination of the people do that for him, and on the whole it may be said that the Provençal legend is the unconscious moulding of facts and reality by popular imagination to accord with their hopes and wishes and prejudices. The legend may be partially or wholly untrue, but it is not a deliberate lie; above all it is not the cunning invention of an individual and his sycophants to impose a fraudulently exaggerated reputation in which he and they share either as dupes or accomplices.

Of course, there are degrees in the legendary beliefs of Mistral's Provence, and they are perhaps worth noting. Confining ourselves for the moment to persons, we may note the first stage in Suffren, a perfectly historical admiral whose abilities and successes were admired even by his enemies; but obviously Maître Ambroise's ballad exaggerates both event and success. We are familiar with this in our own ballad literature. La Reine Jeanne is also perfectly historical, but here the gap between the Joanna of the historians and the Jeanne of the Provençaux is considerable—they are not at all the same person. La Reine Jeanne of legend is simply the ruler that the 'common people' of Provence would have liked to have but never did have. She is the symbol of a common frustrated wish, all the more potent since the actual rulers were the Kings of France—that is, since the death of the bon Roi René—who were thought to continue the destruction and oppression of the hated Albigensian 'crusaders'. She was transformed in time to something like the Kathleen ni Houlihan of Provence, "La Comtesse" who is the symbol of an ideal Provence.

The religious legends are naturally still more nebulous. The arrival of saints or even apostles, at various points along the coast, is certainly not confined to the Saintes Maries whose

84

protection Vincent so warmly recommends to Mireille. St. Tropez, who is confounded with a local St. Eutropius, is said to have been martyred at Pisa, and his body miraculously carried overseas to Provence. His relics are still taken round the town in a boat. At Fréjus the perfectly historical landing in Provence of St. Francesco da Paola is also commemorated by a boat procession, though in fact the saint landed at Marseille and was never in Fréjus. A boat procession commemorates the landing of the Maries and Sara, though according to M. Fernand Benôit the localisation of the legend at its present site dates only from the thirteenth century. How this process still goes on may be judged from the fact that the gipsy custom of plunging the statue of St. Sara in the sea at the two annual pilgrimages dates only from 1935. The gipsies had no Saint. Now they have one of their own, and the devotion is genuine and touching. It is wrong that because they are poor they are not protected from the intrusions of tourists, journalists and *"cinéastes"*. At the time of the procession and mass the village should be barred off by the police, and only genuine pilgrims allowed.

Finally, we come to St. Gens (or St. Gent), who is so much a creation of popular imagination and so suspiciously like a pre-Christian local god in some respects that the Church while not absolutely forbidding the two annual pilgrimages was far from encouraging them. Mistral himself mentions that very few priests or even bourgeois accompanied the pilgrims. Yet Aubanel was much impressed by the procession bearing the Saint's statue, which took place at night and occupied four hours. The bearers went at a run, preceded by a horseman firing a pistol, from farm to farm, where all the inhabitants rushed out to kiss the statue, "weeping, gesticulating, shouting"! A strange cult indeed. St. Gens was one of the rain-making Saints, rather numerous in an arid land, but the famous spring he made in the rock for his mother cured fevers. At his hermitage was a stone trough, called "St. Gens' bed", in which one by one the pilgrims lay, especially girls who wanted to be married. The 'lying' consisted in standing on one's head with

85

legs apart, the girl's skirts of course being held up 'decently' by her friends. The spring dates from the time when the saint's mother came to see him in his hermitage, and arrived very thirsty; whereupon he pressed two fingers in the rock and from one place came wine and from the other water. "Unluckily," say the peasants, "the wine has dried up, but the water still flows and is wonderful for fevers."

In this ambience the innocent loves of Vincent and Mireille unfold, aided by proximity and talk as they gather mulberry leaves for the silk-moth caterpillars.

It is perhaps no more than a personal fancy born of the fact that I admire them both, but the chapter called "Lad-and-Girl Love" in D. H. Lawrence's *Sons and Lovers* has some of the same quality of country-bred innocence and almost unconscious courtship, though Lawrence's over-subtle and self-tormented Paul is the antithesis of the straightforward simplicity and goodness of Vincent. But in neither is there guile or frivolity, any suspicion of the nasty little triumphs of the city-bred male. In neither case is there anything vicious in the lads, and in Mistral's case I think there is no illicit love anywhere in his work.* Mireille is a set-off to her near contemporary of the north, Emma Bovary.

The home production of real silk must have been much more important in the lives of girls in those days than it is now when artificial silk is preferred, for the third book of *Mirèio* is mainly occupied with the chatter of the girls as they wind the threads off the cocoons at harvest time. We are introduced to Taven, the witch of Les Baux; one of the girls betrays Mireille's secret, and at the end we have the famous song of *Magali*.

The introduction in the fourth book of the other suitors for Mireille gives Mistral an excellent occasion to evoke the three main occupations of the Crau and Camargue, the sheep-raising and the cattle-and horse-breeding, all the more interesting since they still struggle on against the difficulties of our times. All three are of great antiquity, though I shall not attempt to give

* Estérelle is married, but the marriage has never been consummated.

86

even the briefest summary of the many learned discussions on these topics. The books of Marie Mauron on these topics are the most pleasantly written and informative to a stranger, particularly *Le Taureau* and *La Transhumance*.

The cult of the bull as part of religious or magical beliefs is older than history, and some most ancient and mysterious relics still exist among the mountains on the frontiers of modern France and Italy. On Monte Bego, at heights between 6,000 and over 7,000 feet, for a distance of more than three miles, the rocks are carved with representations of the heads and figures of bulls or oxen. The Bicknell Museum at Bordighera has copies of about 36,000 of these, an incredible number which at least indicates that the unknown people who made the sculptures must have lasted for many years. Nobody knows who the sculptors were, and all kinds of theories have been advanced to account for them, ranging from the soldiers of Hannibal (who surely had other things to do and would hardly have gone that way at that height) to the compatriots of the Grimaldi skeletons at which we have all peered in the Museum at Monte Carlo. *Quien sabe?* It is a long way from the Camargue, but the existence of the Camargue cattle and horses is certainly established from Roman times. That gives the Camargue *gardians* a chronological start over their transatlantic rivals, the cowboys and *gauchos*.

There do not appear to be prehistoric records of sheep-breeding in the Midi, but the Elder Pliny is said to have noted the use of the caves of Roquefort for the maturing of sheep's-milk cheese in the first century, but I have not verified this. From the point of view of the stranger one of the most curious facts about the Crau shepherds is that they still are, as they have been for uncounted centuries, semi-nomads. In the spring of every year, as the hot sun withers the pasture of the stony Crau, the shepherds lead their charges to the mountain pastures of Dauphiné and the Basses-Alpes, much of the way by the *drailles de transhumance*, rough sheep trails said to be of great antiquity. (The motorist on side roads of Provence and Languedoc will see the notice '*Draille*' warning him that sheep may emerge, and should have priority.) Although many of the flocks are now taken to and from the Alps by train, the traditional migration on foot still continues. In *La Trans-humance* Marie Mauron has given a vivid account of her personal experiences when she accompanied one of these strenuous pilgrimages as a volunteer helper.

It is characteristic of Mistral's intense love for the real life of his Rhodanie that he devotes so much space to describing the occupations and animals of the three suitors and so comparatively little to their love scenes with Mireille. True, their rejection is a foregone conclusion, though one might expect a little more coquetry and kindness even from an unsophisticated country lass who has already chosen her husband. The fact is that Mistral gives eleven stanzas to Alari's flock, five to the cup he had carved for Mireille, and only five to the scene between Mireille and Alari! He lavishes all his art on the description of the migrating flock, such as you may still see in the Crau, led by the first shepherd, who is followed by the sumpter asses carrying the camping equipment and the youngest lambs, the wide-horned goats (supposed to be trail-makers but more likely to destroy the shoots of trees which might invade the pastures), the rams with their special tufts, the great column of bleating ewes and lambs, the rearguard of old and defeated rams, brought up by the second shepherd, with the two sheep-dogs ceaselessly ranging up and down.

Exactly the same is true of Ourrias the *gardian* and Veran the horse breeder—Mistral's enthusiasm for the life they lead and their beasts outweighs his interest in them as characters and actors in Mireille's tragedy. He does not forget his story and his heroine, but he kindles when he thinks of the *ferrades* in the Camargue and the feats of Ourrias in throwing and branding the cattle. He is equally stirred by the semi-wild white horses of the Camargue, which have now lost most of their old economic importance and serve as mounts for the *gardians*. In Mistral's day, when much more grain was grown in the region than now, the horses had a special value, apart of course from their obvious one of mounts for everyone who could afford them. As far back as the thirteenth century the Camargue mares had special privileges in the matter of pasture in the villages because they threshed the grain by treading out the sheaves. "Thou shalt not muzzle the ox that treadeth out the corn," says the Old Testament, but in Provence the horse took the place of the ox for this purpose. It was quite a complicated business and so much associated with the life of the farms that the horses were abandoned for the mechanical thresher as reluctantly as the traditional harvesters from the mountains (the *gavots*) were sacrificed to the reaper and binder.

Naturally the poet's imagination is more stirred by the horses of the Camargue in their semi-wild state than in their agricultural servitude, though he doubtless saw them more frequently at the Mas dóu Juge than at liberty. The horses of the Camargue no longer run wild, though the last herd·is said to have been brought in as lately as 1950—too much of the once open land has been turned into rice-swamps. But it was the sight of these wild horses and the tales he heard of them which inspired Mistral with one of his most famous and poetic passages:

> "Cènt ego blanco! La creniero,
> Coume la sagno di sagniero,
> Oundejanto, fougouso, e franco dóu cisèu.
> Dins sis ardèntis abrivado
> Quand pièi partien, descaussando,
> Coume la cherpo d'uno fado,
> En dessus de si cóu floutavo dins lou cèu.

> "Vergougno à tu, raço oumenenco:
> Li cavaleto Camarguenco,
> Au pougnènt esperoun qui i'estrasso lou flanc.
> Coume à la man que li caresso,
> Li veguèron jamai soumesso.
> Encabestrado pèr treitesso,
> N'ai vist despatria liuen dóu pati salan;

"E'n jour, d'un bound rabin e proumte,
Embardassa quau que lie mounte,
D'un galop avala vint lègo de palun,
La narro au vènt; e revengudo
Au Vacarès, que soun nascudo,
Après dès an d'esclavitudo,
Respira de la mar lou libre salabrun.

"Qu'aquelo meno sóuvagino,
Soun elemen es la marina:
Dóu càrri de Netune escapado segur,
Es encaro tencho d'escumo;
E quand la mar boufo e s'embruno,
Que di veissèu peton li gumo,
Li grignoun de Camargo endihon de bonur;

"En fan brusi coume uno chasso
Sa longo co que ié tirasso;
E gravachon lou sóu, e sènton dins sa car
Intra lou trent dóu diéu terrible
Qu'en un barrejadis ourrible
Móu la tempèsto e l'endoulible,
E bourroulo de-founs li toumple de la mar."

I have an idea that long ago I read a translation of that by George Meredith, but there is no need to look for it since we possess a much better interpretation, or rather re-creation, from the best of our living poets. Roy Campbell is the only English-speaking poet who has lived in Rhodanie as one of the people, earning his living as a fisherman of Martigues or as one of the most successful and popular *raseteurs* in the bull-fights and *gardian* at the *ferrades*. Though Bonaparte Wyse wrote in Provençal and was accepted by the Félibrige on his merits as a poet, in comparison with Campbell he was a dilettante. Indeed there are many native members of the Félibrige who have lived and spoken the language in Provence all their lives and yet have never lived the life of the people as Campbell has. His poem on the horses of the Camargue is an original in the sense that it is built from his own experience and emotion, and the inspiration of Mistral's lines started his poem as it might have been started by a passage of Virgil or Homer. Yet by giving the spirit of the Camargue so vividly it also interprets the lines of Mistral far more accurately and eloquently than any other English version:

In the grey wastes of dread,
The haunt of shattered gulls where nothing moves
But in a shroud of silence like the dead,
I heard a sudden harmony of hooves,
And, turning, saw afar
A hundred snowy horses unconfined,
The silver runaways of Neptune's car
Racing, spray-curled, like waves before the wind.
Sons of the Mistral, fleet
As him with whose strong gusts they love to flee,
Who shod the flying thunders on their feet
And plumed them with the snortings of the sea;
Theirs is no earthly breed
Who only haunt the verges of the earth
And only on the sea's salt herbage feed—
Surely the great white breakers gave them birth.
For when for years a slave,
A horse of the Camargue, in alien lands,
Should catch some far-off fragrance of the wave
Carried far inland from his native sands,
Many have told the tale
Of how in fury, foaming at the rein,
He hurls his rider; and with lifted tail,
With coal-red eyes and cataracting mane,
Heading his course for home,
Though sixty foreign leagues before him sweep,
Will never rest until he breathes the foam
And hears the native thunder of the deep.
But when the great gusts rise
And lash their anger on these arid coasts,

When the scared gulls career with mournful cries
And whirl across the waste like driven ghosts:
When hail and fire converge,
The only souls to which they strike no pain
Are the white-crested fillies of the surge
And the white horses of the windy plain.
Then in their strength and pride
The stallions of the wilderness rejoice;
They feel their Master's trident in their side,
And high and shrill they answer to his voice.
With white tails smoking free,
Long streaming manes, and arching necks, they show
Their kinship to their sisters of the sea—
And forward hurl their thunderbolts of snow.
Still out of hardship bred,
Spirits of power and beauty and delight
Have ever on such frugal pastures fed
And loved to course with tempests through the night.

In spite of all they have to offer her as persons, as owners of property and as men leading more romantic and glamorous lives than that of a basket-weaver peddling his wares round the country, the three 'wealthy' suitors are dismissed, and Mireille remains faithful to her Vincent. In real life, as I have pointed out, the romance would most likely have taken a very different course from that in the poem. Mireille, suitably chaperoned to avoid scandal, would have made a runaway marriage. If the parents had remained hostile, she might soon have regretted the change from the comparative opulence and plenty of the farm to Vincent's penury. On the other hand if he had showed himself the good worker he claimed to be and had been willing to put up with a certain amount of snubbing, he would have been taken to work on the farm, which no doubt he and Mireille in the end would have inherited, to play the same parents' game with their own daughter. But obviously this did not make much of a story. If *Mirèio* had ended with the first four books it would still be a fine poem and possibly unique in its portrayal of the life and characters of Provence. But obviously Mistral intended to go more deeply into his theme, and above all to reveal the stronger passions—whether good or evil—developed in these apparently simple pastoral lives, as well as the legends and beliefs created by their imagination and love of the marvellous.

Much of the fifth book is taken up by the fight between Ourrias and Vincent, and the consequences which carry us far into the cloudy regions of Provençal superstition and sorcery. How far Mistral developed and embellished this supernatural tradition under the pressure of contemporary Romanticism and his own imagination I shall not attempt to say. It may have been—most probably was—much more potent and wide-spread in his day than it is now.

After his rejection by Mireille, Ourrias rides off in a rage, having discovered or guessed that Vincent is his rival, and meets him on the way to a tryst with Mireille. Vincent vanquishes his enemy in fair fight and spares him, but the *gardian* returns and treacherously wounds Vincent with the *trident*—the three-pronged half-moon-shaped spear-head used to tame and drive the bulls. Vincent falls in a pool of blood, and Ourrias flies from his crime back to the Camargue. And here Mistral most effectively brings into play the supernatural. The boat in which the murderer tries to cross the Rhône trembles and begins to sink. It is the eve of St. Médard (8th June), and according to Mistral's poem the ghosts of all those drowned in the Rhône rise from the water and move slowly along the banks, each carrying a light. They are looking for a good deed and an act of faith, for when after many years each has gathered a garland of them, the drowned souls may enter Paradise. But the water floods the ferry-boat under the faint light of the moving ghosts, and Ourrias the guilty is drowned. We are left uncertain whether this speedy punishment came from the ghosts or divine justice, which of course makes it all the more mysterious and terrifying.

What is the origin of this belief and why is it attached to St. Médard, whose name does not appear in the list of saints

93

particularly honoured by the Guilds or 'Communautés'? No doubt it is known, but I have not been able to discover it. The belief in *li trevant* (ghosts) existed in Provence as everywhere else, and in the *Armana* Mistral has a comic story about some lads of Tarascon who planned to frighten a man on his way home by dressing up in white sheets—but he heard of it, himself dressed in a white sheet and frightened the life out of them by silently joining them! The legend of the drowned soul in its present form is certainly Christian, though it may have predecessors in pagan fears of will-o'-the-wisps and wreaths of drifting mist by the river edge. All the country round Arles was full of stories based on the great cemetery of tombs in the Aliscamps, and it is perhaps worth mentioning that the tower of St. Honorat (the ruined church in the Aliscamps) is not a belfry as one supposes but a *lanterne des morts*, a beacon of the dead which was lighted every night. Hence perhaps the association of lights with the *trevant*. The drowned presumably died without absolution, and the mingled piety and pity of the people would explain the invention of this unorthodox opening of the gates of Heaven by the virtue of any of their 'good deeds' and 'acts of faith' of the living.

The evocation of the supernatural is carried still further in the sixth book, which Mistral seems to have designed as a parallel to the sixth book of the *Æneid*. Virgil takes his hero into the underworld and shows him the scenes and phantoms invented by the dreamers of antiquity; and so Mistral brings before us some of the Provençal beliefs in witchcraft, fairies, pucks, and various evil spirits. It must be confessed that the descent of Vincent and Mireille into the Cave of the Fairies near Les Baux is less skilfully motivated than in the Roman predecessor. After lying helpless all night with his wound Vincent is found soon after dawn by three swineherds, who carry him to the Mas di Falabrego, where Mireille naturally is dismayed and horrified to see her lover in such a state. Rather than betray Ourrias (whose fate, of course, is unknown to him) Vincent says he accidentally wounded himself while cutting reeds. Maître Ramon realistically suggests a little brandy (*agriotat*) to start with, but Mireille's mother insists that the wounded young man must be taken to Taven, the witch; and allows Mireille to go with him unaccompanied except by the men, who carry him and then leave Vincent and Mireille inside the witch's cavern.

As if to underline the fantasy of what is to come, Mistral abandons any attempt at realism in his descrption of the magic healing of Vincent's wound. After lying out all night unable to move Vincent had heard Mireille's mother say that the more dangerous the wound the better the witch could treat it, and had been so weak that four men had been needed to carry him to the Cave des Fées. Yet once there, and without any treatment, he is able to walk an immense distance through haunted caverns, faced with all kinds of terrifying phantoms and evil presences, and listens patiently to the witch's long explanations and descriptions, until at last they reach her hearth with its circle of seven black cats, and the wound is healed! Of course it is intentional, for Mistral could easily have solved a little problem of construction like that. Yet it is a question whether this miraculous journey with the witch before the healing of the wound really adds to the mystery. The reader may grow impatient with the witch's endless though interesting explanations of her supernatural visitors as he thinks of the young man's suffering and poor Mireille's anxiety.

How closely Mistral was following popular tradition here rather than his own observation may be seen from the fact that he takes his couple underground at the Trau di Fado, which is at Les Baux, and brings them back *a riverder le stelle* at the Trau de Cordo, which is close to Montmajour, and must be about fifteen kilometres distant! Naturally Mistral had explored both, and knew perfectly well that the popular belief in the "underground passage" connecting them was as much a fable as the hobgoblins supposed to dwell there. His object, one may say, was to show symbolically the fears and destructive passions which lurked even under that southern sun and in lives which in his own words were "sober and patient".

Returning from the underworld, the poem takes up again

the loves of Vincent and Mireille. Urged by his son and
daughter, Maître Ambroise, much against his better judgment,
sets out to ask for Mireille as his son's wife. He arrives on the
Eve of St. John, just as the harvest is to begin, which provides
an occasion for the description of the ritual bonfires, and more
glimpses of the patriarchal life. An excellent description of the
old-time Christmas ceremony and rejoicing was cut out from
this seventh book as a digression. Of course Mistral was right,
but fortunately he printed the banished stanzas in his notes.
They should not be missed, as they are the perfect expression in
verse of the scene of 'Calèndo' which Mistral reconstructed
with such loving exactitude in his Museon Arlaten, the only
place where it can be seen, for the ceremony has long since
died out.

Naturally, Maître Ambroise does not succeed in his hopeless
mission, though he tactfully broaches the subject without
mentioning Mireille, describing his son's passion for a wealthy
farmer's daughter and expressing fears that if frustrated
Vincent may die. Maître Ramon treats this with great contempt, and advises a thrashing, as in the good old days when
parents were respected. But this is nothing in comparison with
the anger and abuse which descend on Mireille from both
parents when she confesses that she is the girl and vows she
will ne'er wed another. Maître Ramon's anger and disdain pass
from Mireille to Vincent's father, who of course resents it, the
two old men angrily compare their war records, and part in
dudgeon. Mireille is first told to go off with her 'gipsy' and
see how she likes boiling a pot under a bridge for supper and
shelter, and then sent to bed in floods of tears. This is one of
Mistral's many admirable scenes of real life and gives the
impression that he must surely have witnessed such a domestic
drama even if he were not one of the actors! Its flawless
realism makes an excellent contrast with the fantasy of the
hobgoblin scenes underground which precede it.

Although there remain five books of the poem, the actual
story is approaching its sad end—which once more points to
the justice of Lamartine's oft-quoted remark about the poem's

theme being Provence. Crying in bed and sleepless, Mireille remembers that Vincent had told her that whenever she might be in danger or trouble she should go to the Saintes Maries and ask their help. The transfer of her instinctive allegiance from the parents to Vincent is well noted. She dresses—which gives Mistral a chance to describe and praise the *costume d'Arles* he admired so much—and before dawn starts off on foot for the old church which stands on the verge of the Camargue and the Mediterranean.

Those who make the 'pilgrimage' today by car from Arles in about half an hour must make an effort of imagination to realise the difficulties—and even dangers for a girl—of the fifty kilometres or so which Mireille must have travelled on foot in two days. Mistral himself made the journey from Beaucaire with a group of other pilgrims in overcrowded carts, and has described it with admirable humour and cheerful acceptance of the difficulties and fatigue, as well as enthusiasm for the old church and the curious ceremony of lowering the relics from the upper chapel into the nave. Mistral's pilgrimage took place in May 1855, and was made part of the way through a heavy rainstorm; Mireille's is at the end of June under the blazing harvest sun. She reaches the Grand Rhône about evening, is given shelter by a fisherman's family, and the next day ferried over the river. She has to skirt the Etang de Vaccarès (now a not too well guarded bird sanctuary) and in that treeless waste is smitten with sunstroke, and is barely able to totter to the church. Meanwhile, of course, the parents have discovered her flight, and learn its purpose from the shepherds who saw the girl pass in the starlight before dawn.

Mistral has been censured for devoting so much space to the story of the Saintes Maries and their miraculous appearance to the dying Mireille, thereby holding up the action of his narrative. If *Mirèio* were a novel there might be some point in this, but it is a poem, and of course Mistral's object is to show how the mingled credulity and imagination of the Provençaux were, in their serious aspects, deeply religious. When Mireille is suffering from thirst on her weary journey she appeals to the

St. Gent I have already mentioned as a creation of popular piety and imagination, and he leads her to a spring. Far from being a defect of the poem, the long episode of the Saintes appearing to Mireille in the church, their story, and her death are handled with great skill. From a purely mundane point of view one might argue that the Saintes do not altogether play fair— Mireille asks them to give her Vincent, and they tell her happiness is not of this world, and therefore the only way in which her prayer can be granted is for her to die and go to Heaven! It must always be remembered that when Mistral is dealing imaginatively with this complex of Provençal legends, both secular and religious, he does so not only from the point of view of a poet but from that of the *païsan* (peasant), which he calls himself in the dedication of *Mirèio*. He is not writing as the educated literary man and philologist who produced the notes where Dante is quoted, the possible Greek origin of some Provençal words discussed, and the scientific names of birds and plants given. He wrote as the peasant-poet he was born, and not as the *savant* which education had made him; or rather, he meant to use his acquired knowledge in the service of the peasant-poet. This refusal to range himself with the 'monsieurs' was deliberate as well as instinctive, showing itself later in his refusal to stand for Parliament and the Académie Française (in both of which he would probably have succeeded), but it is the reason—or one reason—why he was able to write for the people as well as about them. Can one imagine the peasantry reading the cynical 'peasant' stories of Zola and Maupassant?

Although we are not actually told so, the inference is that Vincent when he throws himself on the body of his dead love also dies, or at any rate wishes to die. In any case whether the tragedy is single or double, there is a tragic ending to innocent love, frustrated by social conditions and family prejudice. It is the eternal theme of Romeo and Juliet in another time, country and class. In spite of which inevitably the question was asked (with considerable impertinence!) of Mistral himself—was there a 'real' Mireille in his life? An indiscreet question which of course he smilingly evaded. Now Mistral married late in life, and nobody but a fool will suppose that a handsome, wholesome man would live to be over forty without love affairs. One might appeal in confirmation to passages in *Moun Espelido* or to the opening of the poem *Arlatenco*, written in 1858:

"Vous lou dirai, e lou creirés,
La jouventuro de quau parle
Ero uno rèino, car saubrès
Qu'aviè vint an e qu'èro d'Arle.
La rescountrère un bèu dilun
Dins la palun:
Es grand daumage
Qu'ainsin anèsee à la calour
En acampant de jounc en flour
Pèr li froumage."

(I tell you, and you'll believe me, that the girl I speak of was a queen, for you must know she was twenty and from Arles. One fine morning I met her in the marshes, and it was a shame that in such a hot sun she had to go gathering the flowering reeds for cheeses.)

The poet's premature declaration of eternal love is dashed by the announcement that she is already promised to a *gardian*. It is a light-hearted piece, rather like the shepherdess songs of the medieval Provençal poets. Much more serious and passionate is the famous *Magali* song in *Mirèio*, which is of course based on a very ancient traditional song but given by Mistral a remarkable depth of feeling. And we can link this with one of his last poems (published over fifty years later), the *Tremount de Luno*, where the poet broods over women famous in poetry and in history, but with the recurring refrain:

"Mai, o Magali,
Douço Magali,
Gaio Magali,
Es tu que m'as fa trefouli."

99

(But, oh Magali, sweet Magali, gay Magali, it is you who made me tremble with joy.)* Whatever inferences may be drawn from these and other love poems, they certainly give no support to the theory that Mireille was 'a real person' and a tragedy in Mistral's life. The public is ruthless in its refusal to allow a writer any imaginative gift. Nor is there any evidence (so far as I know) that the death of Mireille in the church after her vision of the Saintes Maries was suggested to Mistral by the story of his friend Aubanel and the fair Zani, who disappointed her lover by deciding to take the veil. It may have suggested Mireille's death, although the Aubanel-Zani affair happened some time after Mistral had begun his poem. There is certainly no hint of it in the speech made by Mistral in 1887 when he welcomed Aubanel as a new member of the Academy of Marseille, and that would surely have been the moment to do so, since he speaks at some length of Zani as the inspirer of Aubanel's *La Miougrano entreduberto*. While some mention of these speculations must be made, the wisest plan is to think of Mireille as part of the youth of Provence and Mistral's own youth. To remain always young in the memory of men she had to die young.

"S'èi de pas qui ié fau, de pas emplissès-la."

(And if it is peace she needs, then grant her peace) is the poem's last line.

As we have already seen, Lamartine's eulogistic article on *Mirèio* introduced the poem to the Parisian literary world, and he was followed by others, including Barbey d'Aurévilly. But praise, even by creative writers, does not necessarily persuade the public to read a book. The fact that only a very few years after its publication *Mirèio* was used by Gounod as the source of a popular opera did much to familiarise the public with the work. The busts of Lamartine and Gounod still occupy the entrance hall of Mistral's house at Maillane, which may be held

---

* Ajalbert says the poet wanted heads of Arlésiennes carved on his tomb saying: "We must remember those who inspired us."

to show that he felt he owed much to their friendship and support. And though at first the Midi was (it is said) less enthusiastic than Paris, Mistral and *Mirèio* soon became public institutions, while of course the Félibrige (which has flourished for a century on gloomy prophecies of speedy extinction) has both supported and lived on Mistral's reputation.

The contemporary success, however, while helped by these exterior and largely accidental aids, must have been mainly due to the poem's poetic merit and to the vivid presentation of a traditional life which most people either did not know about or thought had long disappeared. Men seem always to value a way of life when they have almost lost it. Even when *Mirèio* was first published it dealt with simple characters and a way of life which was being modified by exterior influences. The railway and the substitution of steamboats for horse-drawn barges on the Rhône were as significant of change (and perhaps of the decadence of ancient virtues and qualities) as the substitute of the mechanical reaper and binder for the team of harvesters, and of the steam-thresher for the *rode* of white Camargue horses. Though to some extent idealised, all that Mistral told of Provence and its people in his poem was true—traditionally true even when not actually true, as of course in many cases it still was in 1859. The contrast with the hectic metropolitan life of the Second Empire must have been very striking. Equally so, one would think, must have been the contrast of this truth and simplicity with the factitious and declamatory productions of declining Romanticism.

5

'Calendau'

At this point it seems natural to pause a moment in these notes if only because we have already looked at most of the writing by which Mistral made his work widely popular—*Mirèio*, the songs, the prose of the Almanac and *Moun Espelido*. Obviously that all too short book of memoirs is not so high a literary achievement as *Mirèio* and the other poems, narrative and lyric, but it is the best commentary on all the early work as well as the unique witness to Mistral's intimate life and feelings. Unfortunately the book goes hardly any further than the publication of *Mirèio* in 1859, after which, as he says, the remainder of his life story is the history of his publications, "a matter of publicity". Of course, the exterior facts of Mistral's later life are known, something of his inner life may be found by a study of his work, but after about 1860 we lack the intimacy and admirable good humour of these fascinating personal notes. Perhaps the publication of the *Complete Letters* —there are said to be a great many still unpublished—may compensate, though I doubt it. Not even a great poet can live a perpetual youth with its enraptured discoveries, and probably not even Mistral could have continued the book of his memoirs with the same charm and gaiety. Perhaps the best continuation of his life is to be found in the prose pieces which Pierre Devoluy so admirably selected from Mistral's contributions to the Almanac.

No doubt Mistral was right to mark as the end of his youth the publication of *Mirèio*, which was certainly a contemporary success and has already lasted out almost a century. But it would be a mistake to think that there was no opposition, no hostile and even perverse criticism. There was; though

Mistral, unlike his near contemporary Tennyson, seems not to have been at all disturbed by the would-be cruel and crushing 'attacks' which are the inevitable attendants on merit and success. The *Revue des Bibliothèques* of Avignon attacked Mistral sharply, and complained that one of the chastest of poems had 'painted' the loves of Vincent and Mireille in *"des couleurs trop vives"*! Jasmin naturally could see no merit in the poem. Two periodicals of Marseille jeered at it, and Gélu—whom Mistral in return treated with magnanimity—declared that there were not fifty good lines in *Mirèio*! And went on violently: "I am not a charlatan, nor a 'papist', nor a sacristan, not complicated, nor a lick-spittle, nor a rhymer of twaddle. I'm not a Félibre!" As a matter of fact, though he was a poet, he was really a frustrated socialist with a sore head.

And the opposition did not cease in 1860. A certain Mary-Lafon, who had already returned to the publisher the first parts of Mistral's dictionary on the grounds that the work was incompetent, published in 1882 (when Mistral was fifty-two!) the following intelligent remarks:

"Basically the poem by the young rhymer of Maillane is the expansion of the love-affair of a peasant-girl and a basket-weaver into seven hundred and forty-eight stanzas of seven lines each. The girl's father refuses the beggar-boy, and this new Estelle, who adores her Némorin, rushes off to ask the protection of the Saintes, and dies because in the hurry of getting off she forgot to put on her straw hat to protect her from sunstroke. . . . What possible interest, I ask you, can there be in this bare-foot basket-weaver, as coarse as his own work, and this red-faced peasant-girl, both of them sunburned and smelling of garlic and rancid oil? Literature is an art which, if it is not to end up in mud and manure, must seek its inspiration in other surroundings, taking into account the gains of Progress and the refinements of civilisation."

It reads like a parody, but Monsieur Emile Léonard, author

of an excellent monograph on 'Mistral and the Learned', publishes it as genuine. And, in fact, I can think of people today who would have much the same reaction, though perhaps not quite the same brutal candour of class prejudice. But note how Mistral got it from both sides! He was too much of a 'papist' and lick-spittle for the Marseille Red, and too vulgarly proletarian for the middle-class Mary-Lafon.

Monsieur Mary-Lafon's comment on *Mirèio* has been preserved by accident as a curiosity; but, like every other successful writer, Mistral must have received many others of the kind. And, of course, criticism still continues. As I have already mentioned, the intellectuals of today put up an objection to *Mirèio* as 'folk-lore' and ostentatiously prefer *Lou Pouèmo dóu Rose* (the Poem of the Rhône), which is unquestionably a very fine poem of great eloquence and beauty with an interesting change in Mistral's system of versification; but as a matter of fact the stories of the Drac and the Prince of Orange and all the tradition of the old-time Rhône navigation are just as much 'folk-lore' as Mireille and Magali and the Saintes Maries. In another area the criticism (not to say carping) of Mistral as linguist and restorer of the language still goes on from the point of view of the 'Occitaniens', who in the true spirit of self-determination want to preserve the dialect of a village at the expense of the revived *langue d'oc*. Here, however, the Mistraliens have a much harder position to defend. If Mistral protested against the 'centralisation' of Paris and the imposition of French on the Midi, why should not the villages of Languedoc and Gascony protest against the 'centralisation' of Maillane and the imposition of Provençal? Those interested in this curious problem should read the excellent *La Branche des Oiseaux* by Monsieur Sully-André Peyre, where the problems are stated with knowledge and competence, and solved with good humour.

The fact is that *Mirèio* was a very great achievement which with time and study one comes to respect and admire more rather than less. At one great stroke Mistral achieved the beginnings of the ambitions of his student days. With *Mirèio* he re-founded the *langue d'oc* as a language, not a *patois*, at once literary and popular; he revealed the poetry of the life and tradition of his Rhodanie which nobody before him had had the insight and wit to see; and he invented characters and a story—sentimental, if you like—which have lived and moved people for a century.

The dedication to Lamartine which was added to the second impression of *Mirèio* says of it: ". . . . *es moun cor e moun amo, Es la flour de mis an . . .*" (It is my heart and my soul, it is the flower of my years . . .) And that is literally as well as poetically true. *Mirèio* was the heart and the soul and the flower of his Youth, and he could no more have reproduced that masterpiece than he could have written another set of memoirs of his Youth, another *Moun Espelido*. Any normal person, not carried away by *a priori* theories or prejudices, can hardly fail to respond to the emotional appeal of Mistral's poem, with its love for the country and country life of Provence.

Herein, however, lay and perhaps may still lie a possible cause of misunderstanding in his readers, one from which Lamartine himself, it seems, never got free. By birth Mistral was a peasant like his father, yes, though his father was in fact a well-off yeoman farmer, owning his land and employing a number of farm hands, shepherds and so forth. It is therefore not wholly incorrect to describe Mistral as a 'peasant-poet', provided you remember that his family were in fact landowners, and that he was a highly educated man. A 'peasant-poet' suggests someone such as Charloun, who really was a more or less uneducated poor 'peasant' with a gift of writing popular lyrics to popular tunes. But, as we have seen, Mistral had a brilliant academic career, taking all the prizes at his school, passing his Baccalauréat, and taking a degree in Law. He was a classical scholar, and a great philologist as well as a perpetually active student of the literature and antiquities and history of his country—not just Rhodanie or even Provence, but the whole Midi, and La France, who had no more devoted son. Mistral was that extremely rare person, a writer who was both highly cultured and yet genuinely and by up-bringing in closest touch with 'the people' and able to write both of and for them.

With the passing of youth, this close intimacy with 'the people' faded a little, inevitably, because 'the people' cannot feel that a highly educated member of their community is still really one of them. Already when he came back from his university studies Mistral, as I have related, had found, with distress, that a barrier had been raised between him and the girls and boys of his own age. They understood each other without the slightest need for words. Even in their teens they had chosen their mates. But while they accepted Mistral of course as one of themselves, there was a something between them, a veil, a suspicion. By education he had become a *'Moussu'*. *Pecaire!* he had even written a thesis in French! Almost a *Franchiman* therefore.

Unless Mistral had been a great philologist he could never have created or re-created the literary-popular language of *Mirèio*. Inevitably as he grew older, as his friends came to be chosen from the intellectuals, as his work on the *Trésor* progressed, he lost the intimate touch with the boys and girls of his youth—not wholly, for he always remained sympathetic and responsive, but as his fame and influence grew along with his knowledge, he could not help but drift apart. A man cannot be at once a 'peasant' and the unofficial Comte de Provence, whose word weighed against that of the Republic in Paris. And it is that, I believe, which explains why a poem so wonderful and imaginative as *Calendau* has never taken hold of the people of Provence as *Mirèio* did and does. It may well be that *Calendau* is the finer poem, but it has never touched the heart and soul of Provence like its fore-runner. Even a foreigner can feel the difference. Mireille and Vincent touch us to the heart, but Calendal and the mysterious Estérelle are scarcely more real than the characters of Ariosto. On the other hand we have doubtless come to put too high a value on mere *vérisme* of situation and character in narrative, while fantastic characters were needed to carry off fantastic legends.

Apparently Mistral began work on his *Trésor du Félibrige* in

1862, while he was also at work on *Calendau*. The mere writing work of the *Trésor* must have been enormous, since the MS ran to 14,000 pages. In the course of his twenty years' work he made himself one of the foremost philologists of his time, while he engaged in constant correspondence and took infinite pains to get first-hand information about rare and technical words from the workmen in person. One of his friends has related how Mistral talked with the fishermen of Maguelone (in Languedoc of course), and in turn touched each part of their boat saying: "We call this so and-so, what do you call it?" carefully noting the replies. The same story is told of him at Cassis, and of course Cassis is the home of Calendal in the poem.

This philological work involved also an encylopædic knowledge of Provençal history, legends, traditions, customs, trades and occupations, equipment, furniture, costume—all that he so ingeniously made visible in his Museon. Some of his learned Parisian friends pedantically insisted that this dictionary was too much of an encyclopædia; and wished him to cut a lot of the information he gives. But Mistral could be gently obstinate when he wished, and he quite rightly built his dictionary as he wished and for the purpose he intended—to show Provence and, above all, its poets the wealth of their language. Inevitably this evolution of Mistral from the clever younger son of a wealthy farmer into the most learned Provençal of his time showed itself in his poetry. It would not be hard to show that *Calendau* displays more brilliant and mature poetic powers than *Mirèio*, but the very learning which made that possible tended to cut it off from the people. True, his hero is still a man of the people, a fisherman of Cassis, but Calendal is surely the most remarkable and successful fisherman Cassis ever heard of. And the heroine is no longer the simple country maid of a Mas, she is the mysterious *fée*, Estérelle, who is identified with the Countess Alix of the great House of Les Baux, supposed to be descended from Balthasar, one of the Three Wise Kings, she whose ancestors had numbered among them Emperors of Constantinople, Princes of Orange,

Tarentum and Achaia, Counts of Spoleto and Avelin, Podestàs of Milan and of Arles, whose royal alliances included those of England, France, Nassau, Brunswick, Poland, Barcelona and Provence! In spite of the chastity and propriety of all arrangements, it is really a *Lady Chatterley's Lover* situation.

Why did Mistral take his hero from Cassis, instead of from Martigues, which must have been infinitely picturesque a century ago, and, moreover, was in his own Rhodanie? It is a point I have been unable to clear up. It is true the Martigues fishermen often fish the Etang de Berre, which is a little inland sea, and not the open Mediterranean. Or he may have wished to get away from 'Rhodanie' to another part of Provence. Or it may be that he heard in Cassis the legends about Calendal the fisherman and the '*fée* Estérelle'. From the point of view of contemporary English the choice has turned out rather unfortunate, since at certain seasons of the year Cassis unhappily suggests Bloomsbury-sur-Mer, and any remaining glamour is not helped by the prevailing cement works. Such is the price a poet may pay for being too territorially patriotic in his poems, just as much of Walter Scott and Burns has been killed by the Scotch tourist trade. There are no sacred places left. How wise Dante was to stage his poem in Hell, Purgatory and Paradiso, for which even the American Express cannot sell one a ticket. Another reason for preferring Cassis to Martigues is that there were no lonely hills close to Martigues in which Estérelle could hide.

Fundamentally, *Calendau*, like *Mirèio*, is a poem of Provence first and of its characters afterwards. The difference is that the story of Mireille touched the feelings of the people, while they cared little about Calendal and his princess. And then Mistral abandoned the plain of Arles, which was his life, for the sea and the mountains which were comparatively alien to him. But, in spite of all these hesitations and drawbacks, what a wonderful piece of work it is, and how vividly and beautifully he has carried out his essential plan—the interpretation and revelation of Provence. It may be argued that Calendal should not tell so much so boastfully of his own story, but Mistral had the high authority of Virgil's *Conticuere omnes* . . . books. (This deliberate Virgilian imitation is perhaps yet another indication of the humanist underlying the Catholic.) But the great drawback is in the social proportions—a fisher-lad however brave, attractive and daring doesn't wed the last heiress of the great House of Les Baux by catching 1,200 tunny-fish, winning the water-jousts, overcoming a robber, and even daring her brigand-husband—who is no husband—in his sinister and voluptuous stronghold. Could the last Princess of the quasi-royal House of Les Baux become the wife of the 'consul' of Cassis?

Such, roughly summarised, is the criticism one hears of *Calendau* from readers who are not of the Midi; and though it has much more substance than M. Mary-Lafon's social objections to the loves of Mireille and Vincent, the difficulty is not really serious. In *Mirèio* is the spirit of youth, and its natural spontaneous expression in a love as naïve as it is intense, stimulated by unquestioning religious faith. When she is frustrated in her love Mireille goes direct to Les Saintes, to ask them to give her Vincent. It is an unresolved question whether Mistral intended an irony when, instead of giving her Vincent, they gave her death. In *Calendau* religion is less important than in *Mirèio*, in spite of the pilgrimage of expiation to La Sainte-Baume and other episodes and allusions. Here Mistral seems more occupied in working out a conception of love which may have been suggested by his reading in the troubadours. In any case it is much more complicated and subtle than the simple natural urge to mate of Vincent and Mireille. In *Calendau* the lover must aspire, and the lady must be won not only by perseverance and deference but by a series of more or less daring and always successful actions undertaken for her sake. She controls his conscience. He uses the gains of his catch of tunny to buy her jewels, and sacrifices them by throwing them away when she shows him she does not value money. Again, though she admires his energy, it is evidently Mistral's view that her sense of right and wrong should control it. So, when in a reckless fury he cuts down single-handed the larch trees on

Mont Ventoux, Estérelle does not hesitate to rebuke him for a meaningless destruction undertaken only to display his strength and skill. He instantly acquiesces, and undertakes his pilgrimage of expiation.

One can see why such a story and such a view-point would be less sympathetic to Mistral's Provençal audience than *Mirèio*, but on the other hand a most appreciative French critic of Mistral thinks that *Calendau* was less popular because it is "too Provençal"! Where most readers agree is in thinking that the real strength and beauty of the poem are in the 'episodes' such as the pilgrimage to the Sainte-Baume. In Provençal *baumo* means a cave, and the 'sacred cave' in question is that where Mary Magdalen* is supposed to have ended her days in penitence as a hermit in the once heavily-wooded hills not far from St. Maximin, where the great basilica still shows the saint's relics. Here, of course, Mistral was back in the ancient legendary Provence he knew and loved so well. Mary Magdalen had already appeared in *Mirèio*, since she was one of that considerable number of saints who were in the boat with the Saintes Maries.

Even before the arrival in Provence of the Romans there was a sacred wood in the region of the present Sainte-Baume, with dim traditions of spirits of the dead hunting by night. The pilgrimage of Christians still takes place every July 22nd to the cave, and on the following Sunday to the Church of St. Maximin. It is said that before the Revolution pilgrims brought away as souvenirs some of the Saint's hair or glass rings which had touched the shrine—so irresistible is the desire in these Southern people to have and to hold some tangible symbol of their religious faith and emotion. In these days they have to be content with a little pilgrim's booklet, one of which I have before me. It contains the story of the Saint and her companions, with long quotations (in French) from *Mirèio*, mentions how St. Martha captured the Tarasque at Tarascon, notes some of the most famous pilgrims from St.

---

* She is of course Mary of Magdala, not the 'sinner' who broke the vase of ointment.

Louis (in 1254) to Lacordaire—passing over eight Popes, thirteen Kings and numerous Saints—and gives the recent history of the shrines during and after the Revolution. It omits the well-known story of how Jerome Bonaparte saved the great organ of St. Maximin from the destruction which had been ordered by having the Marseillaise played when Barras came to inspect the place. But it does tell how Barras and Freron destroyed everything in the chapel at the Sainte-Baume, and absurdly changed the name to 'Thermopyles', which the peasants refused to accept. And the peasants seem to have won, for in the French Army Ordnance Survey map it is not marked 'Thermopyles' but 'Grotte de la Ste-Baume'. The booklet ends with hymns to the Saint in Latin, Provençal and French and the "Messe de Sainte Marie Madeleine". In *Calendau* Mistral involves his hero in a battle of the Compagnons, and the power of the Saints and of Calendal's eloquence is showed by their miraculous conversion to peace and fraternity—"*De Santo Madaleno e de Sant Meissemin*".

Yet for some readers the finest section of this long episode is the proud enumeration of the great Roman buildings in Provence, beginning:

"Ansin, esfatant sa bassesso,
Aurenjo, futuro princesso,
Carpentras, Cavaioun, Sant-Roumié, Sant-Chamas,
S'arrengueirèron en carriero
D'arc-de-triounfle . . ."

The poet mentions only the surviving Roman arches of Orange, Carpentras, Cavaillon, St. Rémy and Saint-Chamas, and then goes on to the huge aqueduct bridge known as the Pont du Gard, wisely omitting those destroyed by man, like the three of Arles—the 'admirable' arch, the arch of Constantine, and the unnamed one destroyed so recently as 1839. That five Roman arches, not to mention the arenas and theatres and temples, should still survive in so small an area gives an idea of how far the province was Romanised, and explains the pride with which Mistral in another poem could boast that the men of Provence were "Gallo-Romans and gentlemen."

By way of contrast we may turn to the vivid and animated episode of the tunny-fishing expedition (Chant 5) and for yet another contrast to the equally animated evocation of the traditional pageant Fête-Dieu* of Roi René in Aix (Chant 9) celebrating Calendal's capture of the horrible brigand, Marco-Mau. It might be said, and of course has been said, that these much-admired pieces are really separate poems which rise above the surrounding narrative and would have been more effective if they had been presented as separate short poems. This is really only the old fallacy of the "pure poetry" critics who did not believe there could be such a thing as a long poem —nor can there be if you expect to have it keyed up to lyric intensity the whole way. Every long poem, even the most vigorous epic, has its plains and mountains, but the scenes on the heights gain immensely by being part of a continuous action. Whatever may be said justly or unjustly against the 'fable' of *Calendau*, none of the episodes mentioned or of the many others which might be cited would really be as effective if separated. We have seen how Campbell has made a superb poem from stanzas on the wild horses of the Camargue, but they need their own setting and the background of Rhodanie to give their fullest value.

Of course, in a work of this romantic kind the eventual uniting of Calendal and Estérelle is a foregone conclusion. As in any such book, whether prose or verse, novel or 'epic', it is what happens on the way that matters. It is as certain from the beginning of the *Iliad* that Hector will die as that in the *Odyssey* Ulysses will reach home. Perhaps there was a touch of melodrama in ending with the destruction of the 'Count' and the robber-band in a forest fire, while two thousand inhabitants of Cassis beat out the flames and save the lovers. But, as everyone knows who has seen them, those forest fires are a most destructive reality, and the story of Provence

* Fête-Dieu—Corpus Christi.

would be incomplete without one. It becomes a fitting background for Estérelle's passionate cry:

"O Dièu! O Dièu, suprème asile!
D'abord qu'as fa tant dcfccilc
En aquest mounde bas, l'acès dóu grand amour,
Perdouno is amo trop bouiènto
Que l'entravadis impaciènto,
E que lou sauton . . . E, vaiènto,
Duerbe-ié lou clarun que n'a gens de brumour!"

(O God! O God, our refuge! Since in this low world of ours Thou hast made the gaining of a great love so hard, forgive those over-eager souls who fretting at obstacles over-leap them. To such in their courage grant that light which knows no mist.) Such an apology for desperate lovers' suicide is certainly unorthodox as well as moving. The swift change from that despair to the triumph of safety and happiness makes a dramatic end.

In *Calendau* Mistral greatly extended the scope and setting of his art. *Mirèio* is as carefully limited in area as it is in theme. Anyone with a car can start from Avignon and make for Vincent's home at Vallabrégues (taking in the Abbey of St. Michel de Frigolet on the way), and thence go on to Arles by way of Tarascon, St. Rémy, Les Baux, Charloun's Paradou, Alphonse Daudet's Fontvieille, the Abbey of Montmajour and the Mont des Cordes. It is an easy day's drive with plenty of time for leisurely exploration. The Crau and the Camargue (down to the Saintes Maries) need separate days, as there is no bridge over the Grand Rhône though there is a ferry at Port St. Louis. Anyway, three days suffice, though no mere visit can give a hint of the slowly-growing fascination which comes from unhurried frequentation. Only those who have first 'done' the area in the usual tourist way and then have returned later for a much longer stay will understand what I mean. One should always come to Provence from the north, and not make the mistake of coming from Italy—nothing, not even Austria can endure the comparison with that incomparable land of the Muses.

Calendau takes as its scene the Provence of the sea coast and the mountain. Of course, Les Baux comes in again, and Cassis, Aix and even the Sainte-Baume are easy enough; but much more complicated is the journey of Calendal to the castle of the robber which is supposed to be near the Clue d'Aiglun, in the mountains to the north of Vence. It is quite possible to follow the general line of Calendal's journey and to see the places he saw—a fascinating introduction to a Provence off the main roads to Nice and Monte Carlo. Mistral must have seen all these places and landscapes, which he evokes so brilliantly, though he did not necessarily make that exact journey. Indeed Calendal seems to have diverged from the direct way rather more than we should expect of an ardent lover anxious to have it out with his rival, but there may have been some ancient trail or sheep track he is supposed to follow, though I have not been able to trace it. But Mistral is never wrong about such things.

From Cassis, Calendal made his way through the mountains and over the Col de l'Ange to Cuges-les-Pins (renowned for its crops of capers) to Signes "where love holds its tribunal"—an allusion to the Court of Love allegedly held there by Clarette des Baux. He traverses Méounes, with its lemon trees and oleanders, seeing Roquebrussane and then Brignoles, which last was the summer residence of the Counts of Provence and the place where the Countesses bore their children, perhaps to be at a safe distance from the doctors of Montpellier and Marseille. There is a story about Brignoles (not related by Mistral) which strikingly illustrates the advantages of direct action in politics. Brignoles was renowned for its plums, which were candied and exported in large numbers in the sixteenth century. The orchards belonged to the local Seigneur, and during the religious troubles the inhabitants of Brignoles destroyed all the trees just to spite him; since when the celebrated 'plums of Brignoles' come from near Digne.

The posterity of Brignoles must be grateful to those serious-minded and public-spirited demonstrators.

Avoiding the main road to St. Raphael and Cannes, Calendal then followed the valley of the little river Caramy to Lorgues (passing near the famous abbey of Thoronet) by way of Vins and Carces:

"How many bees in the wild sage, how many small birds in the sumacs! How clear the air! What deep shadow on the mountain-side!"

Passing through Draguignan, he made for Calas and Fayence, but we are not told how he reached St. Auban (or its environs), though in fact there is only one road through that lonely country (by way of Brovès) which crosses the main road from Castellane to Grasse at a tiny place called Le Logis du Pin, which nevertheless now has an inn. Somewhere between St. Auban and the Clue d'Aiglun, Calendal met the 'Count's' hunting party. The road is not easy driving, especially towards the end, but for much of the way it goes through a Provence as different from Rhodanie as from the luxury towns of the Côte d'Azur. The modern who is eccentric enough to visit these depopulated crags and gorges should not miss the well-known Gorges du Verdon.

And of course this is but a fraction of the places Mistral evokes in *Calendau*. The destruction of the larches occurs on Mont Ventoux, the mountain which Petrarch climbed for the sake of the view, the first man to do such a thing since the collapse of Roman civilisation—a feat which was duly rebuked at the time as useless and sinful, for obviously God made the world to be despised and exploited, not to be admired and loved. Again, after the people of Cassis have turned against Calendal at the instigation of his enemy Alphéran, Estérelle tries to console him by telling the story of Guilhem Court Nez and his defeat at the battle of Aliscamps and the scorn of his wife Guibour. This takes us not only to Arles and Nîmes but into Languedoc. Here, as so often, the legend has been shown to contain some grains of truth. Count Guilhem Court Nez was not wholly an invention of the poets, for he really existed. He was a cousin of the Emperor Charlemagne, and his second wife was really called Guibourg (though she was not a Saracen), and though there was no battle in the Aliscamps (the idea evidently being suggested by the vast numbers of tombs in that sacred place) there certainly was a battle not far from Carcassonne in which Count Guilhem's troops fled from the Saracens though the invaders had been so roughly handled they had to retreat. Mistral does not mention it in his poem, but the name and monastery of Count (now Saint) Guilhem still remain (the monastery and church sadly despoiled) in the valley of the Hérault. The cloisters are in New York.

These instances are only part of many which show how widely Mistral extended the scope of his second long poem. That his inspiration remained the same may be inferred from the fervent address to Provence which 'still glows':

> "Pèr la grandour di remembranço
> Tu que nous sauves l'esperanço . . ."

"By the grandeur of your memories, you who kept hope alive for us; you who, in spite of death and the grave-digger, make the blood of our fathers re-live hotter and finer in our young, you who once inspired the gentle troubadours and then made the voice of Mirabeau roar like the mistral; for the waves of the centuries with their storms and horrors in vain wipe out frontiers and mingle nations, since Nature, Earth our mother, always feeds her children with the same milk; her hard breast will always give oil to the olive tree— spirit for ever re-born, joyful, proud, alert spirit! heard in the rippling of the Rhône and its wind! spirit of the music-laden woods, of the deep sun-smitten bays, religious soul of my country!"

Nobody will question the sincerity of that invocation in spite of its rhetoric, but at the same time nobody can fail to notice how it differs from the invocation at the opening of *Mirèio*. True, the poet there speaks of himself first as a "humble student of the great Homer" and then, somewhat inconsistently invokes the Christian God to help him in his humble task of telling the life-story of a peasant girl and "raising her to the fame of a queen". The *Calendau* invocation includes a bitter reference to the Albigensian Crusade and how the men even of Marseille and Avignon came to the aid of Beaucaire and Toulouse "against the black harriers", the "barons of Picardy, Germany and Burgundy."

The tone is quite different, political rather than religious, defiant rather than submissive. If Mireille and Estérelle are to be taken as living symbols of Provence, we cannot avoid noting that Estérelle is no peasant, but the last descendant of a noble house renowned for its warriors. In other words—had not 'Provence' changed its meaning for Mistral between the two poems, and while still including the endless humble life of generations of toilers come to mean a political Provence striving to recover its independence, as Ireland certainly did and Brittany was thought to do? In the summer of 1866, the year in which he finished *Calendau*, Mistral wrote his famous lyric *La Coumtesso* (The Countess), which everyone knew meant 'Provence' as everyone knew that 'Countess Cathleen' meant 'Ireland'. Was Mistral hoping to create a separatist movement which would result in severing Provence from France?

As early as 1861 Mistral had written a poem addressed to the poets of Catalonia, in which he denounced the Albigensian Crusade with even more bitter fervour than in *Calendau*:

"When out of the north came Simon de Montfort, crusading for the glory of God and the law of the stronger arm, when the black ravens, the hungry ravens, fluttered down and tore asunder the nest, the mother and the brood, then Tarascon, and Beaucaire, and Toulouse, and Béziers made a wall of living bodies, O Provence, and you saw them eagerly fly to arms and die for liberty—while today we huddle away at the sight of a policeman!"

117

In 1866 Mistral had met the Catalan poet, Victor Balaguer, who had been banished from Spain as a political exile. And in August of that year Mistral wrote his 'Countess', which begins:

"I know a Countess of imperial race both in rank and beauty, fearing no one high or low, and yet the light of her eyes is veiled with sadness."

And then comes the significant refrain:

"Ah! if only they understood me, if only they would follow me!"

On top of all this a delegation of Catalan poets, including some very politically-minded, visited Maillane in September 1866. It is hardly surprising that the poet's enemies accused him of conspiring against the State, and indeed it is asserted that he and Balaguer went to Paris together, each on his own political and conspiratorial errand, in January of 1867. Napoleon III was to be overthrown, and a Federalist régime set up in France, presumably with a virtually independent Provence. And it even appears that Mistral's patriotism was doubted during the War of 1870.

Now, the expressions just quoted from Mistral's poetry are certainly vehement, even belligerent, but it seems unfair to found such charges and suspicions on them alone. The Albigensian Crusade was disgraced by the most horrible crimes and savagery, and Mistral was right to denounce it; but after all he was dealing with events centuries away. The reference to the contemporary 'policeman' and to 'huddling away' from him might look suspicious to a Napoleonic préfet, but is probably no more than a half-humorous reference to a personal experience. Mistral and Aubanel, accompanied by the painter Grivolas, had been exploring Mont Ventoux, got lost, and arrived in rather a bad plight at a small village, where next morning they were arrested by the local police as suspicious characters lacking the *papiers* beloved of bureaucracy. After a good deal of unpleasantness they were just about to be marched off to jail when most fortunately the curé recognised Aubanel, who of course was official printer to the Holy See in Avignon. The 'suspicious' line about the policeman is therefore probably no more than the poet's protest against the "little brief authority" which sets stupidity over intelligence.

Part of a letter written by Mistral in Paris at that time has been printed, and shows him interested solely in literary matters, except for a brief mysterious postscript which, however, seems to hide a love affair rather than a conspiracy against France and Napoleon. Moreover, it is certain that in later days Mistral refused to stand as *deputé* (when he would unquestionably have been elected) and refused to offer himself as candidate for the Académie Française, preferring his life as the poet of Maillane and to serve Provence in his own way.

The point is more important than it seems, and must affect one's judgment of Mistral, not as a private person or even as an artist but as a 'representative man'. What did Mistral mean by 'Provence'? Of course 'Provence' is one of those abstract, emotion-charged words which meant different things at different times, ranging from a mere geographical expression to a mystical faith symbolised by idealised figures of women— Mireille, Estérelle, La Comtesse, even Nerte and Anglore. But did he also mean by 'Provence' the setting up of a redundant local government, whether independent or part of a French 'federation', a separatist political re-arrangement? If so, the less Mistral he. One of the many blunders of the twentieth century has been the hasty and ill-considered setting up of new little 'sovereign States' cut from the decadence of great ones—with the result that they either fall into impotent obscurity outside the main current of life, or are gobbled up by some large unscrupulous neighbour, and are far worse off than they were before.

When Mistral opposed what he called the 'centralisation' of Paris, for what was he striving? Surely not for a feeble political entity, which would have been no more than Monaco on a larger scale, but for a way of life, for that diversity in unity which is the only answer to the world-uniformity urged by political pedants and stooges for money-grabbers. What Mistral was really opposing was the unholy alliance of Parisian company-promoters and machine-worshippers, for whom Napoleon III and the Third Republic were obedient trustees. The corruption has now gone so far that it cannot be arrested, and the Western world will dree its weird—and won't like it. In Mistral's day there was still hope that all mankind would not be regimented into obedient robots, educated in order that they might read advertisements and be sold things, the superfluous and uninteresting and shoddy productions of the worshipped machines. What is the use of tanks, television, H-bombs, supersonic planes, bulldozers, Cadillacs, refrigerators, self-propelled guns, submarines and artificial satellites to men whose will to live is frustrated and whose instinctive comradeship is exploited and betrayed? Rudyard Kipling said: "Civilisation is transportation." On the contrary, civilisation is that which is transported—civilisation is men, not machines. The other day I was awaiting some friends at Marignane Airport when there arrived one of these large, noisy, aluminium, mechanical box-kites. As it came importantly to a halt, out fussed the huge petrol-supplier, the two step-ladders, the little horde of officials; and, after a pause, from the bowels of this flying Trojan horse there crept a couple of dozen insignificant, undersized drears, typical H. G. Wells characters. Civilisation had been transported!

All this of course can and will be brushed off as violent and absurd. The truth is always violent and absurd to those living under lies. And the truth is that man has sacrificed himself and all that makes life worth living to the cult of machines, and those who think they profit by machines because they 'make money' from them. Mistral foresaw and denounced this, as D. H. Lawrence did just as unavailingly, for this strange doom Man has brought on himself cannot, it seems, be avoided, so blind and obstinate is our love of slavery. The prophet was Samuel Butler, who after being sneered at as a discoverer of mare's-nests was obliterated by the perfidious plagiarisms of Bernard Shaw.

"Day by day, however, the machines are gaining ground upon us; day by day we are becoming more subservient to them; more men are daily bound down as slaves to tend them, more men are daily devoting the energies of their whole lives to the development of mechanical life. The upshot is simply a question of time, but that the time will come when the machines will hold the real supremacy over the world and its inhabitants is what no person of a truly philosophic mind can for a moment question.

"Our opinion is that war to the death should be instantly proclaimed against them. Every machine of every sort should be destroyed by the well-wisher of his species. Let there be no exceptions made, no quarter shown; let us at once go back to the primeval condition of the race. If it be urged that this is impossible under the present condition of human affairs, this at once proves that the mischief is already done, that our servitude has commenced in good earnest, that we have raised a race of beings whom it is beyond our power to destroy and that we are not only enslaved but are absolutely acquiescent in our bondage." (Samuel Butler, 13 June, 1863.)

This is supposed to be a joke or a paradox or the raving of an academic idiot, whereas it is one of the most accurate prophetical utterances ever made—and for that very reason totally neglected. The machines *are* the masters, and the concealed sympathy which exists between the self-styled 'free' governments and their totalitarian opposites is simply a community of machine-worship—what is denounced as Communism is really only a method of ruthless bullying of hitherto unspoiled Orientals and Mid-Europeans into machine-worship. As soon as 'Communism' agrees to allow the 'profits' of the machine to go to 'businessmen' and not just to party members, so soon will 'Communism' become of world-wide popularity; and the machines will reign unchecked over their human slaves.

I do not think that Mistral *consciously* understood and

I

foresaw the situation as Butler did. He couldn't, for the threat was not nearly so close and powerful in Provence as it was in England—though in point of fact Butler made his immensely important statement in New Zealand. But Mistral instinctively saw the danger, the death-danger of mechanisation, though he wrongly denounced it as 'centralisation'. He feared the bureaucrat (who indeed is despicable and detestable) rather than the all-conquering machine. Think of the imbecility of a species which will submit to every sort of deprivation and exploitation in order to create 'weapons' which will destroy them as effectually as their imaginary 'enemies'! Think of the stupidity which destroys all the real gusto of life in order that a pack of fools and sadists shall have too much money, which they can only waste or employ to create more destructive machines! A few days before the moment I now write some two hundred machine-worshippers were killed or wounded at Le Mans, because the machines got the better of the pilots. And what is the response? Not: Smash the lot; but: Bigger and better races.

'Progress' they call it! Yes, comic-strip progress. And it is the fact that 'Super-Man' is actually 'Sub-Machinery'.

Strange that Mistral never noted that the great French Revolution found its supreme expression in a machine—the guillotine.

What is certain is that Mistral made no attempt to advance his ideas by political action whatever his political ideas and ideals were. The nearest he came to such action was that he made "the journey to Catalonia" and, which is much more to the point, made a great success of it. In 1859, the year when *Mirèio* was finished, the Catalans revived their ancient 'Floral Games' (i.e., poetic contests), and the next year, the Catalan laureate Damaso Calvet visited Provence and the Félibres. In 1861 Mistral wrote the Ode to the Catalans which I have already quoted; and in 1867 Bonaparte Wyse arranged a series of fêtes for the exiled Victor Balaguer at Vaucluse, Avignon and Font-Ségugne—which was the birth-place of the Félibrige. A change in Spanish politics restored Balaguer to his native

Barcelona, where he at once planned to acknowledge the cordial hospitality he had received in Provence by inviting the Félibres to Spain. Mistral's handling of this affair showed his customary good sense and moderation. He realised that such a demonstration was bound to be reported in the press of Spain and France, and that if anything went wrong it might easily be ridiculed or seized on by enemies as a pretext to denounce the supposed separatist tendencies of the Félibres. Mistral selected his fellow-guests very carefully, for he wished to give the Catalans as good an impression as possible. He tried very hard to persuade Gaston Paris and Paul Meyer to come, and of course they were then big names in the world of international scholarship. Paris refused, but after much hesitation Meyer at last accepted. Mistral himself, with the rather obscure Louis Roumieux, represented the native Félibres; and Bonaparte Wyse was brought in, not only as Balaguer's host in France, but as a distinguished specimen of a foreign convert; an Anglo-Irish gentleman and a descendant of the Bonapartes. It is worth noting that Roumanille, Aubanel and Daudet all had prior engagements. They must have regretted this when they found what a success was made of the whole affair by the generous enthusiasm of the Catalans, and the tact of Mistral and Meyer.

The three Félibres started off humbly enough from Perpignan in the *diligence* for the Spanish frontier, where, to the amazement of the other passengers, they were received by a delegation of excited poets. It will be remembered that Mistral's father had been a soldier in the French Army which besieged the great fortress of Figueras. A mass was celebrated in his memory, and later Mistral recited his Ode to the Catalans, taking great care to stress afterwards the loyalty of Provence to France and of Catalonia to Spain. And well he might, for the Spanish Government treated the visitors as princes. They travelled by special train and in the Queen's own carriage, and were greeted officially by representatives of the Sovereign. Barcelona received them with flowers, speeches, banquets, poems, and—it is said—"the applause of the fair sex". Meyer made a great hit by discovering in a monastery a magnificent Bible which was inscribed by its former owner, Charles V of France, with the date 1388; and offered to buy it for fifty thousand gold francs. Before returning to France the Félibres visited other places in Catalonia, including the famous monastery of Montserrat.

From this interchange between Provence and Catalonia, Mistral and Balaguer, came the famous 'Coupo Santo' which is carefully guarded by the successors of the original Félibres and used as a loving-cup at their banquets. It was paid for by a public subscription raised in Catalonia, and first used at St. Rémy at a banquet where Balaguer was the guest of honour. In his speech he declared grandiloquently:

"Our hearts are one! In ancient times Provence and Catalonia exchanged their troubadours and their destiny. Don Ramon Béranger was born at Barcelona and was the best of the Counts of Provence. Jaime the Conqueror was born in Provence, and proved the best Count of Barcelona. The same waves which break against the rocks of the Château d'If whiten with their foam the reefs of Montjouy!"

To which there was obviously but one reply:

"Provençau, veici la coupo
Que nous vèn di Catalan:
A-de-reng beguen en troupo
Lou vin pur de noste plant!

Coupo santo
E versanto,
Vuejo à plen bord,
Vuejo abord
Lis estrambord
E l'enavans di fort!"

(Provençaux, here is the cup which comes to us from the

Catalans. One by one let us drink from it the wine of our own growth. Sacred and plenteous cup, pour out abundantly, in waves, the enthusiasm and energy of the strong!)

It is one of those occasional poems which are perhaps more acceptable when sung than said.

6

The 'Trésor'

When Mistral returned from this enjoyable poetic jollification in Catalonia, he was still a comparatively young man in his late thirties, with forty-five years of life before him, years of steady unhurried work, with marriage and the companionship of old and faithful friends, and the consolidation of his immense prestige among his own people of the Midi. He had the *Trésor* to labour at for a long time to come, his lyrics to collect, polish and add to, his tale of *Nerto* and the poetic play of Queen Jane to write, and, above all, the remarkable poem of the Rhône which his intellectual admirers generally agree on thinking his finest work.

Yet from the point of view from which this imperfect tribute has been conducted, his greatest achievements—with the exception of the Muséon Arlaten—had already been made. He had found an ancient language persecuted* and in decadence, and like another Dante had by the strength of his poetic genius raised it from a condition where it was sneered at as a *patois* to a poetic tongue of acknowledged beauty and variety. He had succeeded in grouping and keeping together a set of poets—the most difficult of creatures to govern—who were united by devotion to poetry, love of their province and its speech, and above all by their admiration for his genius. It is the genius and memory of Mistral which have kept the Félibrige alive and united for a century, in spite of the perpetual croaking that "it can't last" from outsiders.

It has lasted, and whatever its dissensions and faults and shortcomings—and what human institution is without them?—the Félibrige has been a civilising influence and a means for

* Children in the State schools were punished for speaking it.

126

promoting good will and the love of life for its own sake in many persons of very different social and economic strata. The speeches may be too long, but the fraternal feeling is genuine. It is an antidote to our century of hate, in its own restricted sphere. The great and unforgivable sin of Modern Culture—if I may personify a system and an attitude—is that it teaches its votaries to set themselves apart from and above their fellow-creatures, to despise all who do not wear its livery and talk its jargon. Thus, in spite of its immense and unquestionable attainments, Modern Culture reaps the disdain and even hatred it has sown, and may even be in some danger, if not of ignorant destruction, at least of being driven into academic cloisters with no medieval charm about them. The gap between what is now called 'popular' and 'academic' may grow impassable instead of being bridged by understanding and good-will. The people cannot be learned, but they are not therefore to be despised; yet they must learn that the life-values are not to be found in company-promoting, or in 'social security', or in the perverse cult of machine-worship.

The great achievement of young Mistral—the Mistral of *Mirèio* and the early lyrics and early contributions to the *Armana*—was that in the nineteenth century he produced poetry of very high quality from the life of the people about him, without any kind of condescension or vulgarising, and made something to which the people themselves responded while the best of the intellectuals acknowledged and enjoyed its merits. When Goncourt noted in his journal that Mistral and the Félibres composed "troubadour-like poems" he simply revealed the fact that he could not have read either the troubadours or the Félibres, or both. The poetry of the troubadours centred on the brilliant and aristocratic life of the great families of the Midi before the crime of the Albigensian 'Crusade', and if the 'people' entered it at all it was mainly in the form of a 'shepherdess' whose *raison d'être* was to be melodiously seduced. The poetry of the Félibres was essentially of the people, at any rate in its origin.

Admittedly Mistral and his associates had a comparatively

easy task. Their brilliant revival of the *langue d'oc* was in itself an *argumentum ad hominem* with their potential audience, who by the fact that they knew Provençal were the less likely to have been corrupted by the journalism of Paris. As Coleridge foresaw in England, the spread of popular 'education' tended at first rather to lower the standards of journalism and literature than to raise (as had been so confidently hoped) the intellectual and moral standards of the people. It came of a simple-Simon, too optimistic and 'liberal' confusing of the mere mental machinery of reading and writing with genuine culture. And of course it cannot be stressed too often that the philanthropic object of many influential supporters of popular education was simply to sell things, which was admirably achieved by teaching the people to read advertisements and journalism which persuaded them they had to buy what they didn't need. The retort to the millionaire newspaper proprietor who clamours for 'education' was made by Molière— *"vous êtes orfèvre, Monsieur Josse."* And where would the politicians be without it? as Mr. Tony Weller so sagely remarked of death and the undertakers.

Even so recently as twenty or thirty years ago, in the less exploited parts of western Europe one could still verify that the so-called 'illiterate' peasant had often a much more genuine culture than the journalism-soaked town proletariat. The peasant had better manners, and living as he did the life-ritual of the Church had little vulgarity of feeling. His conversation was more interesting, for it concerned realities he knew and the infinite fantasies of the imagination. When he did read, as was the case with the more prosperous, he read one or two books thoroughly. According to Mistral, as I have said, his father read only the Bible, the *Imitatio*, and *Don Quixote*, though it is curious to hear that a Roman Catholic farmer was allowed to read the Bible. But, assuredly, a man who read those three books and nothing else could not have a vulgar mind. Montaigne thought that there should be a law against inept and unnecessary writers, like himself. And doubtless modern government is right when it labours to suppress them, and to protect its dear friend, the newspaper. Yet I cannot help feeling it was a sad day for England when the upper working-classes abandoned Shakespeare and the Bible for the newspaper and the movie.

One can see all along what Mistral was aiming at, especially when he helped to found the *Armana Provençau*. Although he had taken high academic honours, he saw from his own home life that book-learning is comparatively unimportant and nothing much to boast about. Culture is a matter of right feeling and right adjustment, not of knowing the names of the Merovingian kings and "how many genes make five".* But the spread of 'enlightment' obviously threatened the culture of Provence even in the 1850s, and I infer that the Provençal Almanac was started and continued mainly with the idea of giving the people of Provence something 'journalistic' to read which was not simply disguised commercial or political propaganda from the wire-pullers of Paris.

Countess Martinengo-Cesaresco has unintentionally left us a valuable little anecdote. After relating inaccurately, with a rather British condescension, the story of the Tarasque in her *Folk-Songs of Provence*, she goes on to say that she lunched there with "the Radical deputy for Montmartre, the ablest exponent of political positivism," Monsieur Clemenceau; and told him what she had picked up on the subject:

"Monsieur Clemenceau listened with a look of such unmistakable concern that I said, half amused, 'You do not believe much in poetry?' The answer was characteristic. 'Yes, I believe in it much; but is it necessary to poetry that the people should credit such absurdities?'"

Obviously, if the credulity of the people was wasted upon the Tarasque they would not have enough left to believe in Radical politicians. Which did more harm to France and Provence—the Tarasque or Clemenceau? What would Mistral

* I steal this joke from a well-known Londoner, who may denounce me as a plagiarist if he wishes.

have said if he could have followed the story to its end? Might he not have suggested that it is better for the people to believe in the Tarasque than in politicians who lead them to slaughter and destruction, and then elevate themselves on a pinnacle of glory by assuring the people that under their auspices the nation had just lived its finest hour?

Of course, it may be and indeed has been said that Mistral was opposed to 'Progress'. But what is meant by Progress? That there shall be ever more and more human beings, particularly of one's own nation, living longer, travelling faster and farther to enjoy a more and more uniform and standardised world, imbued with a fanatical superstition of machinery, living in flimsier and uglier houses filled with more and more objects produced by machines, which are purchased by working ever shorter hours for bigger money, rendered all the more necessary to purchase yet other objects to fill the hours of vacant leisure, and nourishing a sturdy patriotism to persuade or compel less happy peoples to pay heavily for the ever-increasing surplus production of the master-machines, while bureaucrats with straw in their hair rule, and calculate the wealth and glory of a nation, not by the quality and attainments of its people but by publishing graphs of their ever-increasing production and consumption. Theoretically, happiness may be pursued by all, but who has caught it, and who shall say what is happiness? I knew a man who at parties and after dinner always urgently questioned his friends: "Are you happy? Are you happy?" and if you said "No," he insisted on your having another drink. Is this the peak quotation of civilisation? After all, even the most despicable tribes of savages find felicity in fuddling. What people call happiness is mainly what happens to be in fashion at the moment. People who do what they really want to do are apt to cause surprise. Thus it is related—I know not if truly—that Beatrice and Sidney Webb celebrated the exultant joy of their union by spending their honeymoon in the British Museum working on industrial statistics. I think they were *crétins*, but I admire their independence.

Change there must always be, though change is not necessarily for the better. Even in his youth Mistral can hardly have imagined that he could preserve Provence from the ravages of the industrial revolution, though of course in that then remote province a century ago he may not have realised that he had something much more formidable than a Tarasque to deal with. The forces being released, the interests and habits being created, were obviously far too powerful to be resisted by the age-old hand-toiling ritual of farmer, craftsman, fisherman and horseman. The thing has now so far worked itself out that men are faced with the alternatives of imminent self-extermination or abandonment of the fetich of irresistible 'Progress' with its unacknowledged assumption that we are really the slaves of our own machines and not masters of our own destiny.

It seems most unlikely that Mistral ever precisely worked out the situation. He was no Samuel Butler peering accurately into the future with a cynical laugh. Mistral's attitude was rather the reaction of the Conservative who sees all that he values in life menaced by forces beyond his control. In any case, when he and his friends were young men Provence was threatened by an economic crisis, into which we need not go, but for various reasons the old-time cultivation of cereals in his district was ceasing to be profitable, and the rice-culture in the Camargue was not started until the War of 1939–45. In his earlier years Mistral may have believed that some form of regional independence would save Provence from the dangers he felt were threatening it. In speaking of *Calendau* I accepted the interpretation of Estérelle as the symbol of Provence, which seems to be true of Mireille and Nerto and Anglore and la Reine Jeanne—all the heroines of his long poems. But I hesitated to accept the very generally credited opinion that in *Calendau* not only does Estérelle represent Provence but 'Count Servan' the robber baron represents the France to whom she is unwillingly tied, while Calendal is the young society of Félibres who intended to rescue her!

Now either Mistral is in contradiction with himself or that

interpretation is exaggerated, or at most means that he hoped the Félibres would free Provence from the French influences which were vaguely but conveniently denounced as 'centralisation'. As early as 1861 in the eloquent poem which he addressed to the Catalan poets Mistral had very clearly stated his position:

"Now it can be seen, now we know that all is for good in the divine order. We men of Provence, one flame, are frankly and loyally part of the great France; as you, the Catalans, are part of great-minded Spain. For at last the stream falls into the sea and the stone into the heap. During the dangerous cold time of the Equinox the wheat survives best thickly sown, and when the air is dark and the wave inky, small boats sail together to sail in safety. It is good to be numerous and to be called the children of France, and, when we have spoken, to see the spirit of a re-birth flow from sun to sun on the nations, and to see God's hand shine from Solferino to Sebastopol. But when the stormy days are past and the steersman sings at the helm, and the sea has calmed, then every ship at its whim takes its own course, to cast its nets or to follow its star."

That surely is clear enough, and sufficiently *chauvin* to satisfy even Louis Napoleon, who was destined to lead France and Provence into a great disaster. Two years after the visit to Catalonia and nine years after that poem was written came Sedan and the fall of the Second Empire. Now, on the vindictive but as it proved exact principle of the revolutionary separatist Irish that "England's disasters are Ireland's opportunities," that surely was the moment for Mistral—if he had really been all along plotting a political independence—to summon his Provençaux to revolt and set up a Count or Countess of Provence? With Paris besieged, the Army of the Loire facing the Germans, a provisional government at Bordeaux and the Commune about to threaten Paris, that surely was the opportune moment? A rebellion in Provence might not have succeeded in the long run, but it would have been as dangerous as the Vendée to the First Republic and have given Bismarck an excuse to send his cavalry to the Mediterranean. Of course Mistral may have changed his views under the shock of the disaster, but he was far indeed from trying to profit by France's misfortunes, and both his *Penitential Psalm* (written in November 1870) and one or two letters which fortunately have been printed show that he felt like any other Frenchman and that his 'separation' was a moral, spiritual and practical repudiation of the standards of Paris. Notice what he says in the *Psalm*:

"Lord, we have strayed from the old ways and laws, we have destroyed the virtues and customs of the home.

"Lord, giving an evil example we denied You like pagans, we closed Your Churches, we laughed at Your Christ.

"Lord, we left Your laws and sacraments unkept, and like brutes put our faith solely in self-interest and Progress . . .

"Lord, France and Provence have sinned through forgetfulness; forgive us our trespasses, for we repent our wickedness.

"Lord, we would become men. Set us free! We are Gallo-Romans and gentlemen, and walk erect in our land."

Fine as the whole poem is, the sentiments just quoted might be those of almost any disconsolate patriot after a national defeat and humiliation, particularly if he has been listening to war-time sermons and reading the editorials of some moralising *embusqué*. As a matter of fact, it is not true that success in modern warfare depends upon the practice of antique Christian virtue by the population in the immediately preceding epoch— who, for example, would claim that the dazzling victories of young Bonaparte were the result of the austere piety inculcated and practised by Barras and his *citoyens*? 1870 was simply one more example of victory going against the Pope's friends. But however much Mistral's lines may betray the illogicality of most war-time thought, they certainly do not emanate from an anti-French separatist. Those who try to prove he was just that do him as great an injustice as those who tried to involve him in propaganda for a quite impracticable restoration of Monarchy, even though he did sit as a Monarchist in the town council of Maillane.

Confirmation of this is given by extracts from letters written by Mistral during that period, which fortunately have been published. Somebody in Paris (it sounds rather like Renan) had said that France was 'finished' but that so long as Progress continued the Prussians might just as well lead as the French— which naturally roused Mistral's angry opposition. Again, after the Commune he wrote indignantly:

> "We are the only people who deny our traditions, and are urged by our governments to impious hatred. For eighty years we have been constantly told that France began its existence in 1789. Hence the gross ignorance of the public and its contempt for history. Our present revolutionaries have just wiped out the epic of the Empire and, what's more, have made the memories of 1792 ridiculous."

This must have been meant as a repudiation of the Communists, and could hardly have been more definite or more devoted to that continuity of living tradition which makes a nation. It is an amiable inconsequence in this indignant French patriot that in the same paragraph he deplores the Revolution of 1789 and exults over the Republican victories of 1792! Patriotism is tolerable while it remains an emotion, and not always then. It is quite intolerable when it becomes a pedantic system, as it did in the hands of fanatical doctrinaires of politics such as Charles Maurras.

Even in the dismal days of 1871 Mistral did not lose hope, and in these letters we find him saying:

> "France cannot die; fortunately she still has too many country folk for that. As a rule nations only end when the fields are abandoned. But I think that it is all up with urban and Parisian dominance."

There is a good deal of wishful thinking in that, and the propositions enunciated are certainly disputable from some points of view; but he is really only repeating in other words his passionate desire to preserve the traditional life of Provence from the disintegrating influences of Paris and industrialism. It is certainly an irony of Fate that the most beautiful coast of France was even then developing a series of picturesque fishing ports into so many Paris-sur-Méditerranée!

To all which, and not with the intention of making confusion worse confounded, let me add that Mistral was suspended from the town council of Maillane from September 18th, 1870 (a fortnight after the fall of the Empire), until January 21st, 1878. And in 1875 Mistral wrote to Alphonse Daudet these extremely energetic words which I despair of translating adequately:

". . . la tyrannie de la démocratie actuelle qui, si rien ne la crève, fera des Latins un peuple de goujats, de coquins et saligauds."

(. . ."the tyranny of contemporary democracy which, unless something smashes it, will make us Latins a race of blackguards, crooks and pigs.")

It would be interesting to know what Mistral meant there by that very vague and claptrap word 'democracy'. After all, universal suffrage is just one more system, and probably no more uncertain than Bridoye's system of settling problems by throwing dice, or our own eighteenth-century system of pocket boroughs tempered by Court bribery of Members of Parliament. Possibly he gave it one or more of its extended meanings which include the liberty to say and do anything which is entirely approved by a great majority, and have since been made to sanctify the substitution of quantity for quality, of the machine for man, of mediocrity for intelligence, of money-pleasures for mind-pleasures. Here was a Mistral who had evolved considerably from that hot-headed youth who in the Revolution of 1848 had been ready to put on a red sash and dance the *Carmagnole*, and might have compromised himself politically but for his father's good sense.

The parallel evolution of Mistral's work has already been noted, while we may even trace a 'social' period in some of his dedications. The first edition of *Mirèio* bore no dedication, and the second and all later editions were inscribed to Lamartine in literary gratitude. Similarly, *Calendau's* dedication paid an old debt to Adolphe Dumas. But when we come to *Nerto* (1883), we find indeed that the Prologue is inscribed to his wife, but Book 1 to the Queen of Roumania, Book 2 to the Countess of Toulouse-Lautrec, Book 6 to the Countess of Gasparin, Book 7 to the Venetian Marchioness Maria Licer! Rather a change from Mireille and Magali. However sincerely Mistral may have intended to go on writing "for the people", it does not seem that after *Mirèio* and some of the songs they really responded to his poetry. He kept in touch with them through the Almanac and his many public appearances and eloquent speeches; and of course his personal prestige and influence—in spite of enmities and envies—went on increasing to the end. The 'popularity' of his early work—one cannot stress it too often—came from the fact that it was written for those who worked the land by one of themselves. *Mirèio* especially abounds with little realistic touches of true life on the land which no city-dweller, smitten with a sentimental love of Nature and man in a state of 'innocence', could possibly have achieved. Ourrias, the witch Taven, the malicious remarks of the girls silk-spinning, are there to show that Mistral knew the life was not all idyll.

In any case he was never a proletarian writer, like Gélu and Jasmin, both of whom mistrusted and were unfair to him, probably for that reason. And the range, subtlety and power of Mistral's art could never command the instant response of the poor in spirit as did the naïvely touching poems of Charloun, who humbly solicited approbation by composing his poems to the tunes of popular songs of the day. Probably many of those who sang Charloun's words did not know they were his. The 'people' are curious in their jealousy of anything which indicates any personal superiority in activities where they cannot compete, even song-writing. It is said that in the last century a song would swiftly pass from village to village and valley to valley of Tuscany and for a time be sung by everyone, though nobody knew who had written it. "If we knew," the peasants confessed, "we should not sing it"!

In his old age Mistral's thoughts returned to his youth and his parents and all that vanished life of his Rhodanie, and he produced in his prose memoirs what some think is his most attractive and accessible book. But it could hardly have been 'popular' with the land-workers of the 1900s. Much that Mistral dwelt upon with the tenderest humour and regret would have seemed to them merely out-of-date and inferior, while all along the more sophisticated reader enjoys (like the author) the striking contrasts between this rustic origin and the Nobel Prize winner, the uncrowned king of Provence!

In the jargon of today Mistral's father would be written down as a rich 'kulak', and his name would doubtless figure on more than one secret list for liquidation and pillage. He was able to give his son a first-class education (though it seems Mistral was greatly bored by the period when he had to read in the Law Schools of Aix University) and even more serviceably left him the modest but certain income without which his long and honourable literary career would have been impossible. So far as I know, Mistral never had to write a line for money and never did—it is the crucial distinction between the moneyed literary artist and the working hack. And obviously from the very beginning Mistral was no ordinary peasant, as Lamartine thought he was. Those who in early days tried to palm him off as "the young peasant-poet" (as if he had been a semi-illiterate, and what he had written was only remarkable as coming from a person grievously handicapped educationally and financially) did him a disservice. There is a story, no doubt apocryphal, that after the publication of *Mirèio* Mistral went into Paris to call on a famous though poor poet who had praised him highly. The poet opened the door of his flat himself and on hearing the name exclaimed indignantly: "What! A peasant-poet from the

Midi who is named Mistral and writes about rustics in Provençal, comes here dressed like a gentleman in a top-hat and speaking university French like a scholar? Where are your goatskin breeches and your sabots? You must be an impostor!" And shut the door in his face.

No doubt this was meant as a Parisian joke (if it ever occurred) not in particularly good taste; but the misunderstanding was natural, and even now persists. The foreign visitor to the museum house at Maillane (from which most of the books and some of the best furniture have been moved to the Muséon Arlaten) finds a pleasant but modest dwelling and an unassuming interior (except for the lapidary inscription put up by Maréchal de France Pétain) and naturally infers a rustic *petit rentier* with literary gifts. It is rather hard to make such a visitor understand that Mistral, on top of his superb poetic genius, his *bonhomie*, his love of Provence and its people, was also a very learned man, a *savant*, on his own ground; though of course he was never 'an intellectual' in the modern sense, which really means a 'sham intellectual'. He must have devoted many years of unhurried but concentrated work to the study of the Provençal language, and to the innumerable subjects, historical, traditional, religious, superstitious, 'folkloriques', technical, proverbial, literary, popular, which such a study must cover. We make a fuss, and no doubt rightly, about Dr. Johnson's dictionary, but Mistral's Provençal dictionary was a greater achievement, for it was not only a dictionary but a reconstruction of a language added to an encyclopædia of Provence. Both Mistral and Johnson had nothing to show for their labour but a financial loss and some vain praise, but Mistral had an unearned income, and Johnson had nothing.

It is another irony that this immense and devoted labour, which, whatever the 'Occitaniens' may say, really did reconstitute Provençal (or the *langue d'oc*) as a language, helped to cut Mistral off from the people, in the sense that he ceased thereby to be one of them and a 'popular' poet. All human beings are conceited, especially saints and the humble, but just

138

as the conceit of 'intellectuals' is based on over-valuing the knowledge they think they have, so the conceit of the 'people' is based on despising the knowledge they know they haven't got. Part of the greatness of Mistral is that in spite of the estrangement he did not lose his prestige and influence—one must stress and repeat this curious fact. No mere highbrow ever achieves a fraction of Mistral's personal intangible power. He was D. H. Lawrence's "natural aristocrat", Plato's "kingly man". It seems strange that he wasn't murdered, but then the nineteenth century had not read De Quincey.

However that may be, the fact is that concentrated labour on this great task kept Mistral steady, sane and serene during the dreadful epoch for all Frenchmen which followed Sedan. The disaster and the inevitable isolation and comparative loneliness which resulted seem to have stimulated him to greater efforts, though it is true that during that epoch his creative work must have been abandoned except for the occasional poems we find in *Lis Isclo d'Or*. He must also have had more time for his dictionary work since during those bad years the social and traditional life of the Midi seems to have been suspended. There can have been few or no occasions for him to make speeches, none of the traditional gatherings for him to attend. I find a curious confirmation of this in an old Almanac in *langue d'oc* published in Sète in 1897. The water-jousts there are supposed to date from the foundation of the town by Colbert in the seventeenth century, and in a long list of names of annual champions I find that no jousts were held in the years 1870–72 inclusive. If the water-jousts were abandoned in Sète, then the life of the Midi must certainly have been paralysed! And, being suspended by the One and Indivisible Republic, Mistral did not even have to attend meetings of the town council.

He is supposed to have started work on the *Trésor du Félibrige* about the end of 1861 or beginning of 1862, though of course he had unconsciously been training himself long before for the task; and then he must have had a genuine interest in in philology, however much some of his purely technical work in that line may now be criticised. If we assume that he began about January 1861, then he took about forty-two months to reach the middle of the letter C. Between August 1863 and March 1870 (six and a half years) he advanced as far as the letter N; yet fifteen months later he could announce he was just about to attack S, and by January 1874 his first draft was finished, though a year's revision lay ahead. Thus, the first two-thirds occupied over nine years, and the last third less than four; from which one may perhaps infer that he was able to give more time to the work in those years. Or perhaps the work already done and the skill which comes with practice enabled him to move faster.

The publication of the *Trésor* occupied the whole of a decade of Mistral's life, though of course not exclusively, since in that epoch he published *Lis Isclo d'Or* and *Nerto*, re-organised the Félibrige in 1877 and got married in 1876! The difficulties seem to have been partly technical and partly material. From the enormous quantity of his script arose the purely technical problem of how many volumes it would make when finally set up in type. The Seguin brothers of Avignon undertook the work, and the decision was made to issue it in parts (*fascicules*) which could be bound up later, but the trouble with that plan was that subscribers could not be informed what the total cost would be. However, in August 1877 Mistral managed to count the lines in his MS and, calculating from a page or two set up as specimens, estimated he would need 1,800 pages. Two large volumes. He had hoped for a government subsidy, but that was now most improbable while he was still under political suspicion, and then he had the additional vexation and trouble that his learned friends in Paris (whose aid seems to have been essential) wanted the great work produced according to their ideas of what a dictionary should be, and not according to Mistral's. And when the publication in parts was well under way, M. Mary-Lafon (the critic who thought Vincent and Mireille too ungenteel to be the heroes of a poem) returned his copy to the publisher on the ground that in the first two letters alone a great number of Provençal expressions were omitted and a great many scientific terms hitherto unknown had been included. Mistral patiently and magnanimously explained. Doubtless there were many other disagreeables, drawbacks and delays, for the publication of the *Trésor* was not completed until 1885, more than twenty years after Mistral had begun to work on it.

Like other great and permanent works the *Trésor* brought no financial compensation to its maker. Towards the end of his days Gibbon calculated that he had received £6,000 (gold) for his history and had spent the same amount on collecting the books needed, so that he received nothing for the literary labour of his life. Mistral fared rather worse, if anything. If he kept his accounts exactly, he received 44,427 gold francs and spent 47,524—which left him 3,000 gold francs (about £375 of our money) out of pocket. Fortunately the 'centralisation' of France carried with it some advantages which appear to have been overlooked, among them the wish and the ability to honour and to compensate men of letters on a scale which could hardly be expected of a province. In 1861 the Académie Française had recognised *Mirèio* and in 1884 awarded the Prix Vitet to *Nerto*. And then, in 1890, a great effort by Mistral's friends in Paris resulted happily, and the Institut de France (not de Provence!) honoured the *Trésor du Félibrige* with the Prix Jean Reynaud, worth 10,000 gold francs—at least £1,200 of our money. The *Trésor* is not the kind of work that money can buy or money can compensate, for it was a labour of love and the consecration of a lifetime's devotion. But it is pleasant to think that Mistral was not left out of pocket, and above all that the well-deserved reward came not from the Comtesse but—from Marianne.

I shall not be guilty of the absurdity of passing judgment on a great technical work beyond my competence, but content myself with quoting two of the many expert opinions which I have noted in the course of considerable reading. The first is taken from an erudite work published half a century ago by Dr. J. Auroze, who says of the *Trésor*:

"All the dialects of the langue d'oc are represented; every word is noted in all its meanings, with examples selected from the best modern and mediæval authors. A poet, even when he is at work purely as a philologist, Mistral refuses to consider the word apart from what it represents, the object, the custom or the action as the case may be. He shows it still living in the proverbs or sayings gathered from the people."

Even if we did not have the testimony of Mistral's friends who actually saw him at work gathering or verifying his linguistic material among the people, we should feel the truth of this from the work itself. No doubt there are other dictionaries equally founded on scholarship and the living speech of the people, but though the great work so evidently is based on the people, it is not so evidently addressed to or accepted by the people, whatever may have been asserted by propagandists:

"While the peasants, shepherds and poets of Provence thank Mistral for having rescued the speech of their ancestors, there will be everywhere, from Paris to Calcutta, wherever men are concerned for the marvellous Latin idiom, readers who will study the pages of the *Trésor*, and will derive from it perpetual enlightment on the mystery of races, languages, and bloods."

I leave that 'bloods' (*sangs*) in its crudity. The quotation is from Charles Maurras, who was about the worst thing which happened to Mistral. The whole statement, like so many from its author, is more to be noted for its self-assurance than its accuracy. How did Maurras know that the "peasants, shepherds and poets of Provence" had even seen the *Trésor*, let alone approved of it? Consider. The book had to be published at 120 gold francs (about £15 of our money, while a second-hand copy today costs about £25), which was an impossible sum for poor men.

About 1900, a cabby of Tarascon earned forty francs a *month* and free lodging. The poverty of the people cannot afford such luxuries, and in any event they see no need for them. They speak as their mothers and mates speak, and the mere possession of a dictionary is a sign of bourgeois contamination. Maurras, as usual, is making a quite unsupported statement for the sake of effect, and getting away with it because nobody tripped him up. It is the common trick of the propagandist journalist.

However that may be, there is surely a vast gap between telling in verse the traditional life of 'Rhodanie' (or 'Rouan-nesse'), linked with the naïve loves of Vincent and Mireille, and receiving in recognition of a Provençal-French dictionary (said to contain 100,000 words) a most important prize from the most erudite public body in France!

7

Marriage and 'Nerto'

France (and Provence) recovered from the calamities of 1870–71 far more rapidly than most people at the time thought possible. Indeed, many of the spokesmen from the foreign Press and Pulpit (who without knowing it shared Mistral's view that military defeat was a punishment for Sin) seemed to think that France had been let off far too lightly and were even inclined to question the inappropriate benevolence of Providence.

As for Mistral—he had in those days personal sorrows, or at any rate distresses on account of his friends, in addition to those of his country. Before the war—in 1869—he must have received with something near consternation the news of a quarrel between Roumanille and Aubanel which made bitter enemies for life of his two closest friends, both of them among the original seven Félibres of Font-Ségugne. Naturally, an event so painful and scandalous has been left in silence or barely hinted at, except in periodicals and in one or two books on Aubanel. No precise motive, so far as I can discover, is given for the break, though it is easy to see the differences of class and temperament which might in the end separate men who had been such close and affectionate friends that in a poem signed by them both in 1855 they said:

> "Surely, we enjoy each other's company, happy and laughing, as if we were a couple of lovers, for, as everyone knows, Roumanille and Aubanel are friends, two friends such as are rarely seen!"

But see the differences. On the one hand Roumanille,

144

educated indeed, but the son of poor gardeners, who began to write verse in Provençal because his mother knew no French, who spent years of poverty as a junior schoolmaster and then proof-corrector, who despised all art which was not solely for the people, a rigid Catholic bordering on bigotry and frequenting very few who did not share his views, and that in spite of an admirable *bonhomie* and humour which glow in his prose tales. On the other hand Aubanel, Catholic indeed, but far from censorious, a cheerful soul whose last book of poems is frankly entitled *Girls of Avignon*, the descendant of master-printers, a born collector of pictures and all kinds of artistic *bric-à-brac*, as much a 'comfortable' bourgeois as Roumanille had been a stinted peasant. There is a letter written by Roumanille in 1869 which says:

"Our relations have taken such an unfortunate turn—and I don't know exactly why—that for a month now Aubanel has failed to visit me, and cuts me."

Only five days later, Aubanel wrote sadly to another friend:

"Lately I have suffered one of the bitterest griefs I can remember. A friend of a lifetime has thrown me over in the most paltry and painful way—a friend who had been like a brother to me. In the first moments of suffering and indignation I wrote a sonnet of anger—I who hitherto had written scarcely any but love sonnets:

The Spider

To a traitor

"Since you will have it so, unkind! since you have broken an old friendship which was so strong, so tender and so easy; since against me you have followed tortuous ways like a mangy dog, some stinking animal! I slam my door and lock it against you. Away with you, traitor, away! Our friendship is dead: you have killed it . . ."

These be bitter words, and leave us wondering what

'treachery' can have provoked them, for the alleged denunciation of the *Girls of Avignon* as indecent by Roumanille to the Archbishop could not have occurred until sixteen years later. What did Mistral do about it? Obviously he must have done his best, have used all his influence to try to bring about a reconciliation between two of his best and oldest friends, whose enmity was a disaster for him and the Félibrige; and obviously he must have failed. It says much for the power of Mistral's influence and even more for the vitality of the ideas inspiring his Félibrige that it was able to survive such shocks, for as late as 1909 there were demonstrations of dissident poets against the contemporary *Capoulié*, Pierre Devoluy, at the annual banquet of the Ste. Estelle (which for some reason he insisted on holding at St. Gilles contrary to some people's wishes), demonstrations which degenerated into a riot, in which Mariéton, it is said, had a tooth broken by a punch in the jaw from a peasant-poet! No wonder Mistral found such events deplorable.

In 1872–73 we find him appealed to in distress by another of his comrades of Font-Ségugne. Alphonse Tavan, only three years younger than Mistral, was a landless peasant labourer but at that time (1854) described as proud and gay. A poem of his, *Li Frisoun de Marieto* ('Mariette's Curls') had particularly pleased the Félibres. He had known a period of happiness after his marriage, but by 1872 he had indeed fallen on evil days. His wife had died leaving him an only child, who some four years afterwards died too. Overwhelmed by grief, oppressed by solitude and poverty, Tavan naturally turned for sympathy to his *Capoulié*. The two letters Mistral wrote are remarkable from more than one point of view. Here is the first:

"Maillane, 26th November, 1872.

"My poor Friend,

"I share to the full the dreadful suffering which has cut you to the heart. The mother was taken from you, but left the child to console you; and now the child in turn has taken flight. Blessed are they that believe! Thanks be to God, for them is left the hope that in the kingdom of Christ and the Virgin Mary they will again see in person those whom they loved. All other consolations are useless, and I earnestly desire that religion will come to help you in the vast grief which darkens your life. It is moreover the one joy you can give the two guardian angels who so prematurely left you. With all my heart as a man I grasp your hand. F. MISTRAL."

No one can fail to perceive the deep feeling which inspired that letter, and the wish to recommend sincerely the only consolation which the writer thinks effective. But evidently Tavan was not to be consoled. It is a pity that, if they exist, his letters to Mistral have not been printed so that we could see exactly what were the distresses he was trying to alleviate, for it is little enough that words can do for the broken-hearted. But the essential may be inferred from the second and longer letter Mistral sent his friend:

"Maillane, 11th March, 1873.
"Yes, I understand, my good friend Tavan, and feel deeply that there is nothing in the world worse than to lose those we love. The death of the person who loves leaves less bitterness than the death of the beloved. Happy are those who go first! To you I must surely seem a happy man, yet I say to you from the depths of my heart—happy are those who go first!

"I wish I could soothe your wounds. But what can I do? I hear that you have lost the faith of your childhood. If that is true, then your misfortune is a dreadful one, for nothing on earth can aid a man whose horizon is bounded by the grave. But if it were so, why should we grieve that the wife and daughter you loved have returned to the eternal charnel-house we call Nature? They feel nothing, they hear nothing, and your grief is as useless as that of the madman who should weep over dead leaves or lament the pebble lost in the stream. If, on the contrary, you have kept that admirable

Catholic Faith which explains everything and makes everything endurable, then I must tell you that you are very wrong to give way to despair. Those chaste, pure spirits which expanded before your transitory love to give you a glimpse of divine felicity are now in the world of truth and light. Like the cicada they have left their outer wrapping on earth to sing on the tree. Why weep for them? They are not to be pitied, they are free and immortal. That divine belief, revealed by the words, miracles and death of Christ, shows you a wonderful path towards them—prayer. Pray, for the God of our fathers has declared that prayer helps the poor dead. Pray and take courage; be pure, be patient and resigned, if you hope one day to be worthy to meet again the two who have left you. What can you hope from the brutal materialism which covers the mournful society of today with darkness? It can bring you nothing but despair, agony, rage and misfortune. The works of the greatest reformers, the republics of Solon and Lycurgus, of Plato and Brutus, fell to ruin as complete as the empires of tyrants, and more quickly. There is only one truth (which is shown by all history), which is that this world is 'a vale of tears', a purgatory. What madness for those whose bodies are subject to sickness, age and death, to try to make this world a paradise. . . . . You complain that you are poor. A great poet, one of the greatest poets of this century, Lord Byron, who had fame, fortune, beauty, was seized while still in his thirties with such a loathing for the world and above all for humanity that he deliberately sought his death in Greece. . . . Become a Christian again, become a Catholic again, and you will recover peace and hope. I am keeping your touching poems for the Almanac, and I hope they will not be the last. I hope very much that you will come to see me. Only, remember to warn me four or five days ahead, so that I don't make any other appointments that Sunday. Come, come, pull yourself together, remember you are not a woman, and that you need strength to keep going to the end. I send you the embrace of friendship. F. MISTRAL."

Surely that is altogether admirable and warm-hearted whether you believe what he says or not? It is the perversity of 'criticism' to ignore the noble humanity of those words in order to enquire whether Mistral himself believed all he wrote, and if so, why did he not practise it? Now, Mistral did say of himself that he was not religious, but superstitious like a good many poets—and his writings to a considerable extent bear him out. It does not seem a very sound argument to maintain that because Vincent and Mireille have an intense simple faith, therefore Mistral must have shared it. You might just as well argue that he had the homicidal impulses of Ourrias or the robber-baron morals of the Count in *Calendau*. The creator of characters must be allowed his freedom. Moreover, there is an instructive little anecdote which seems to be fairly well authenticated. A pious pilgrim to Maillane, going round the church with the curé, asked if he might see "the Master's prie-Dieu"; and received the brisk answer: "He hasn't been to church these forty years!" Another more confused tale shows Mistral buying a crucifix when he was a very old man, because he felt it would not be proper for him to die without having one in the house.

Even if all this is true it does not in the least take away the merit of those two letters. It may have been a case of 'Do as I tell you, not as I do,' but most obviously Mistral knew what was the only possible course for Tavan in his misery and solitude. The letter is not a stereotype, and he might—and certainly would—have written very differently if the person to whom he was writing had been Alphonse Daudet, let us say, or Professor Meyer—both friends as close to him as Tavan, if not closer. In writing to Tavan as he did, Mistral was not a hypocrite. He had been brought up a Catholic and remained one always at heart, but that is not quite the same thing as the unquestioning faith he urged on Tavan, which Mistral must have known was really what Tavan needed and wanted. In any case, the value of the letter is not theological, but lies in its humanity, its sincerity and its fraternal sympathy. There is not a phrase in it which suggests condescension or patronage, nothing to suggest that the letter comes from the great poet and 'uncrowned king' of Provence to a poor working man in his desolation of grief. Talk of the Recording Angel dropping a tear—if Mistral ever needed a Last Judgment plea, he would only have to show those two letters. At any rate, Tavan did not die of despair in 1873 or do anything rash. Perhaps it was through the influence of Mistral that he found better work, and it must surely have been Mistral who arranged for publication of Tavan's poems in 1876 and 1900. Tavan lived on, and died in humble retirement in his native village of Châteauneuf-de-Gadagne in 1905. What was the tragedy of Tavan's life was but an episode in Mistral's, but it shows in him a warmth of humanity and generous sympathy which make any display of ecclesiastical pedantry inappropriate. Who was it said that God should be worshipped in spirit and in truth?

We come to more cheerful scenes with Mistral's marriage and the publication of his short poems under the title of *Lis Isclo d'Or*, the latter in 1875 and the former in 1876. It seems strange that Mistral should not have married until after his forty-sixth birthday, but such is the fact. For over twenty years he had made his home with his mother in the 'House of the Lizard' at Maillane, and he now built just beside it the house which is still piously preserved as Madame Mistral left it in their joint memory. But Delaïdo Poulinet, who had met and married Mistral's father in such a romantically pastoral way, was now growing old and perhaps more in need of care than able to give it. Mistral's marriage seems to have come about far less romantically, and in fact to have been arranged as at any rate a possibility before he ever met his bride, if we may rely on what he says: "On the Tuesday after Whitsun I shall have my first interview with her who is to be my Estérelle, if God so wills." This surely implies that there had been talk of marriage before they had ever met? In any case, Mlle Marie Rivière was not a Magali of Arles, though her family (according to Mistral) was Provençal and 'illustrious'. Her father came from Vienne, which strictly speaking is not in Provence but in Dauphiné; and she had been brought up in Dijon.

Whatever the suspicions of Mistral's orthodoxy he must have complied with the rules for once, since he and Mlle. Rivière were married in the Cathedral of Saint-Bénigne at Dijon on September 27th, 1876. Notice the date. In view of Mistral's superstition about numbers and particularly in favour of '7', one would expect this event to take place on the 7/7/77. But perfection is not of this world, and clearly the lady had the right to "name the day". Either Mistral pleaded for or she allowed the 7 in '27th' and she could not avoid that in '1876'. According to the old Roman calendar and indeed in our own for centuries, the year began in March, so that 'September' as its name implies was '7tembre' and gave him a third good augury. The marriage seems to have been successful as far as it went, for there were no children. One would like to learn more about her than the many gracefully-turned compliments of Mistral's friends. In 1877 he urged a friend to marry, adding "if you only knew how happy one is when one meets a good, intelligent and pleasant woman." He told Daudet that she was the incarnation of Mireille and Estérelle, and wrote yet another friend that she was "charming, beautiful and eager for great and heroic things."

In his old age she was evidently everything to him if we may believe Jean Ajalbert, who writes:

"Casual visitors, dazzled by Mistral, tended to give no more than polite attention to the silent and self-effacing Madame Mistral. They knew nothing of the mistress of the house beyond her timid grace, her charming sweetness, her clear gaze and her fresh complexion. But Madame Mistral was the high priestess of the Mistral cult. Her very keen intelligence made her a most shrewd judge of those many who came to him, and she was at once her husband's adviser and his vigilant defender against intrusions. How tactfully she managed to shorten dull conversations! How careful she was to bring his scarf or his wrap when the evening grew chilly! Above all, she maintained the ambience of simplicity and harmony, in which she was aided by the maid, 'Marie-du-poète', the faithful servant of the house, whose devoted frankness, respect, and free expression of opinion helped the patriarchal simplicity and grandeur."

Ajalbert, though a Parisian journalist and a follower of Goncourt, was a zealous and serviceable friend to Mistral, particularly when political wires in Paris had to be pulled, but he was writing during her lifetime. There is his testimony for what it is worth. We can at least infer that Madame Mistral did not neglect her husband.

In the year before his marriage Mistral collected and published under the title *Lis Isclo d'Or* the best of the short poems he had written during a period of more than twenty years, for one of them is dated as early as July 1853—that is, before the poet's twenty-third birthday. The book as we have it today differs to some extent from the edition of 1875. There was an autobiographical introduction, later cancelled, but reprinted in 1906 in the *Discours E Dicho*, which has never been republished; but the important parts were all reproduced, almost verbatim though expanded, in *Moun Espelido*. The only importance of this detail is that it shows Mistral, as early as 1875, fully aware of the immense influence on his life as an artist exerted by his parents and the particular ambience in which he was brought up. Great men are often in later life— after forty, say—deeply interested in their parents, not for the Freudian reasons, but because they realise how profoundly they have been influenced not only by their heredity but by the personalities of their parents. Mistral's relations with his father and his mother were particularly close. It is hard to say which of the two was the more important. The 'critics' bitterly censure the 'intrusion' of the famous 'personal note' already quoted:

"Coume au mas, coume au tèms de moun paire, ai! ai ai!"

But what could be more truthful than that poignant cry of regret?

On the other hand, we can see the devotion of Mistral to the young mother, who must have been thirty five years younger than her husband. There are dozens of examples, from which we may once more quote the occasion of the prize-giving when Mistral was a schoolboy. The audience of parents was more and more impressed as prize after prize was won by the same boy, who instantly took wreath and book and laid them in the lap of the handsome young peasant woman in the costume of Arles, who accepted them with simplicity and pride. And, moreover, Mistral did not take a wife until he was forty-six. What more could she ask?

Of course there was no reason to retain this preface of acknowledgment to his parents after publication of *Moun Espelido*, which is one of the most touching tributes ever paid by a famous son to comparatively humble parents—in worldly rank, that is, for in other respects they were obviously on a high level. How right, then, that they should have been evoked at the opening of the finest book of short poems ever published in Provençal, and I do not think we need to make an exception of any of the medieval Provençal poets, wonderful as some of them are. Their comparative monotony and artificiality, especially those of the *trobar clus*, cannot endure comparison with the variety and spontaneity of *Lis Isclo d'Or*.

This variety, apart from all its other merits, adds to the difficulty of saying anything pertinent about a collection of miscellaneous poems written in many different moods and on different themes. There comes suddenly to me the desire to show, as a first 'exhibit', an example of Mistral's literary magnanimity, a rare virtue unfortunately in the 'irritable race'. The reader will not have forgotten Jasmin, the barber poet of Agen, and the haughty, not to say provocative, message he sent to his young colleagues of Provence when they invited him to the 1852 congress at Arles:

"Tell them they can gather by the forties and the hundreds, they'll never make the noise in the world I've made on my own."

Even at the time, Mistral and Roumanille were not offended, understanding a poor man's solitary pride; and far from bearing any grudge Mistral recited a charming poem in his praise when in the spring of 1870 Agen honoured the memory of its humble poet:

"To-day is a triumph for the nation, and for our brothers who remain in their country and follow the plough and speak the language of their soil. That is why a son of Provence comes from the folk of Provence to pay our tribute to the great poet of the South . . . Jasmin . . . who sang of love more tenderly than a woman, who moved our hearts with deep feelings, Jasmin, who moved us to tears . . .

"*Avèn vist Jaussemin nous tira li lagremo . . .*"

And then, turning to the end of the book, we come by way of contrast on one of the peasant anecdotes which instantly recalls the old Scottish poem—which may indeed have come from Provence in the first place—"Get up and bar the door".

A shepherd quarrelled with his wife, who was a little sharp and obstinate:

"Suddenly she screamed at her husband furiously, 'Shut up, you lousy . . .' 'Me lousy? Say that again, and I'll break your ribs.' 'Lousy!' Hit in the face with the back of his hand she got up sobbing 'Lousy!' 'What! Isn't that enough for you?' 'Lousy!' Whereupon he grabbed her, in spite of her scratchings, tied her to the rope and let her down the well. 'Now what do you say?' 'Lousy!' He let her down to the water edge. 'Now what do you say?' 'Lousy!' He lowered her to her knees, to her waist and to her chin; the demon of a woman still said: 'Lousy!' In his rage he let her duck under the water, and do you know what she did? She put her two hands out of the water and made the gestures of someone cracking lice! All the shepherd could do was to

154

pull lιⅇ uut. And so when women have the last word we always say: 'Ah, the lousy shepherd's wife.' "

This is nearer to Mistral's *Armana Provençau* manner than to the poet of Mireille and Calendal, but it is proof of his genial versatility, especially when you recollect all the beautiful lyrics in the same book as well as the poems of other types. Turn from the example of ancient peasant ribaldry I have quoted to the long poem on the death of a harvester, possibly part of the long unpublished poem written before *Mirèio*. It cannot be said that here Mistral hides the harsh realities of the poor man's life in 'Rhodanie'. It is as realistic as any of Wordsworth's presentations of peasant life as it actually was (and not as the city-bred poets pretended) though without Wordsworth's piety and platitudes. The tone of Mistral's *Meissounié* is at once stoical and tender. The old leader of a batch of harvesters, unable to maintain the speed of his work, is accidentally and fatally wounded by the sickle of a strong young man immediately behind him. There is nothing conventional in his reaction to sudden death, no false pathos. "Don't weep," he tells the women crowding round him, "better sing, perhaps, with the young men, for I have ended my task before any of you." And he likens himself, in a long drawn-out simile which it is unfair to call 'Homeric', to the old ram who at last is killed by a young rival while the ewes neither knowing nor caring go on cropping the grass. There Mistral touches a hard but salutary truth, the indifference of Nature, and indeed of its own kind except the very few directly concerned, to the death of any living thing, particularly one who has lived his span— even a human being. Mistral at once and rightly alleviates this bitterness with the tears of the women and even the harvesters present, but the real turn of the screw comes when the dying man's thoughts turn to the little olive garden he has planted—may St. John spare the young trees in the heat—and to those who will suffer by his death:

"Up there on the mountain-side, alas!, my family expects

the little money which I brought them back every year.
. . . But now, at Christmas, they will eat without me . . .
O Monseigneur St. Jean, watch over my daughter, console
my little wife, foster my son . . ."

Obvious enough, no doubt, but when deeply felt such a
passage is surely the core of human experience and of poetry
itself, and the answer to the disdainful highbrow assertion that
all the great themes of poetry are entirely worked out and there
is nothing left to write about but one's own metaphysical
subtleties. True enough for the self-important intellectual
who has never lived, but Europe has had three thousand years
of poets who did live, and will have more. If *"dins tout soun
orguei Lou siècle mor d'enuie"*—if with all its conceit the age
perishes of boredom—that does not mean there will never
again be men who live natural lives and feel and express the
poetry of real existence.

I must not linger too long over this book which contains so
much of Mistral's life and of the life of Provence. An English
reader may perhaps grow impatient with its defensive praise of
the Provençal language, and ask: Do English poets ever make
such a fuss about the necessity of writing in English? No, but
they may have to, under the threat of a vast new *patois* which
tries to destroy native English as certainly as the Franchiman's
tongue tried to destroy Provençal. Let us remember how
Gaelic in the eighteenth century and Erse in the nineteenth
century were persecuted languages. And already from the
point of view of a minority we can begin to share the feelings
which created such poems as the *Coupo*, the *Coumtesso* and even
Lou Lion d'Arle. No doubt there is a good deal of patriotic
mythology about that Arles lion, who is supposed to have been
petrified in the rock above St. Rémy after having ruled so long
over the "Gulf of the Lion", which, in spite of Mistral, was
probably the gulf of the 'lonns' or lagoons—the same Celtic
word which is in Mague*lone*. The feeling is genuine enough,
as it is in the poems for 'Noces', a *genre* Mistral rescued from
the most deplorable conventionality by making the situation

real and genuinely rejoicing in the happiness of his friends. Genuine too are the enigmatic and for once personal love poems which open the section called *Li Plang* (the laments) which ends with the Elegy on the death of Lamartine. There is no clue to the subject of these love poems except a reference to Uriage, which is a little watering-place close to Grenoble. The poems are undated. And that is all one can say, except to praise them as poetry, which after all is the essential.

The last poem I shall cite from this collection is the ode *A La Raço Latino* which I have already quoted, since an extract is inscribed on marble near the Peyrou at Montpellier where Mistral recited the poem to a large out-of-doors audience on May 23rd, 1878. During the same festival of the *Santo Estello* he delivered an impassioned prose oration on the 'Provençal Renaissance'. This poem is far from being the only place where Mistral evokes and praises the 'Latin race', whose existence he takes for granted. It must be admitted that this is one of the occasions where Mistral is on rather uncertain ground, at least from our point of view, though in our time the conception of 'race' has become more a matter of political prejudice than of cool scientific investigation. As a child I remember studying with much interest the photographs (though not the text) of two large illustrated volumes, *The Races of Mankind*—or some such title. Perhaps prejudices acquired from this premature but wholly superficial study are what prevent me from agreeing with Julian Huxley and others that there are no races of mankind. Of course you can easily juggle the scientific definitions and evidence to make it appear that there are no races. But just as in the species dog we all recognise unscientifically at a glance such varieties as a pug, a poodle, a Newfoundland and a Peke, so I don't think we ever confound a hairy Ainu with a Hindu or an Australian 'abo' with the Pope. The experts arrive at their learned dubieties by measuring cephalic indices, examining types of hair, and so forth. But the impressive pilosity of Alphonse Daudet, for instance, does not seem to be racially linked with the egg-like appearance of Gabriele d'Annunzio. However un-

157

scientific and common-sensical the approach, there do not seem to be any marked and common traits by which members of the 'Latin race' may be instantly distinguished by anyone from other Europeans. Obvious facts to anyone who has frequented the western Mediterranean region are that the populations in the bigger ports are genetically very mixed, while the uncrossed stocks in the mountain regions belong to very different types, local types. In short the conception of a 'Latin race' seems a fragile basis on which to build a 'Renaissance'. I don't know from whom Mistral picked up the idea— Gobineau, perhaps—but it was eagerly taken up some of the many contending doctrinaires who were trying to draw Mistral in their direction. It is best to think it a poet's dream when he tells the 'Latin race' in the poem recited at Montpellier:

"The Pantheons were willed with the pure forms of your women; all hearts responded to your triumphs and your tears; when you flower the whole earth is in flower; everyone charmed by your whims; and when your glory is in eclipse, the whole world is in mourning!"

Tell that to the Nordic blonds, while if the aborigines of the Americas could have recorded their opinion they would have expressed bitter regret that the 'Latin race' had ever come in contact with them.

Still, a story is still told in Montpellier about Mistral's visit which shows the 'Latin race' in an amiable light in contrast to the virile races which revere only force and money in their innumerable forms and disguises. On that May day of 1878 Mistral drove in an open carriage from the station towards the Peyrou, and of course had to pass through what is now the Place de la Comédie. In those days it had not become a roundabout for endless cars and noisy lorries, so that the cafés still had orchestras, and many people enjoyed sitting out on the *terrasses*. As Mistral's carriage passed, everybody stood up, the men raised their hats and cheered, and the bands played the *Coupo Santo*. This might happen in Germany but hardly in

England, where the poet's public ovation is usually postponed until the day he is safely buried in the Abbey.

All the evidence goes to show that, whatever a few more or less fanatical camp-followers said and did, Mistral's purpose was to keep his Félibrige as far as humanly possible clear of disputes, polemics and demonstrations, political and religious, and it does not seem possible that his rhapsodies about the 'Latin race' implied any stirring up of the racial hatred which has been so shamelessly fostered and exploited by political adventurers. This is clearly shown by the articles of association of the re-organised Félibrige of 1876. The original Félibrige of 1854 was the outcome of the spontaneous enthusiasm of seven poets, most of them young, who wanted to express their faith in themselves and each other and the ideals they professed. How many groups of young writers have done the same, before and since, only to find in a few years that one or two have succeeded, the rest have more or less failed, and the *mouvement* is forgotten? Only three of the original seven really succeeded, and it is doubtful if even Roumanille and Aubanel would now be much read but for Mistral.

It was Mistral who saw that in his cleverly named 'Félibrige' —which could be made to mean whatever seemed to serve poetry and the people of Provence—he had hit, perhaps unintentionally, on what could be made a powerful and enduring organisation. One of the fallacies of our epoch is the illusion that organisation is everything, and spirit and truth nothing. So long as you have an elaborate paper plan with statistics, the people don't matter, and if they lack enthusiasm— bully them into pretending it. The Félibrige had started with enthusiasm, spontaneously, and had grown so fast that by 1876 Mistral realised that the original simplicity was outgrown, and a more formal organisation was needed. We can see his influence at work—and amusingly—in the fact that the 'Consistoire' was to be made up of seven times seven members! The object of the Félibres is defined as "the uniting and fostering of those who by their works preserve the language of the *pays d'Oc*, as well as those scholars and artists who study and work in its interest." The most essential paragraph is one which forbids the Félibres to discuss topics of politics or religion or culture likely to cause dissensions or divisions—much the same as an officers' mess if you added women's names. The new organisation provided for the holding of *Jeux Floraux* every seven years, when the poet laureate was to receive his wreath "from the hands of Beauty"—i.e., a pretty girl in the costume of Arles. The invitation to form local 'schools' of poets was received with remarkable alacrity—who would have thought the old land had so many poets in it? The names are so picturesque I am tempted to quote some of them: In Aix-en-Provence, the *Soucieta di Félibre de Lar*. (I suspect a touch of Provençal irony in that title. 'Lar' is the name of the river near Aix, which the Franchimans, disdaining the *patois*, to this day wrongly inscribe on their maps as 'L'Arc'.) In Alès they created the *Soucieta di Félibre Gardounen* (allusion to the river Gard); in Marseille, naturally *L'Escolo de la Mar*; at Nîmes, *La Miógrano* in compliment to Aubanel; at Avignon, *Lou Floureja*—and so forth. The most interesting and productive of all these subsidiary 'schools' is the *Nacioun Gardian* founded in the first years of this century by the Marquis Folco de Baroncelli, which brought the Félibrige back from the Café Voltaire to the hardships and solitudes of the Camargue—and produced the poetry.

An old building with a tower in the village of the Saintes Maries de la Mer contains a tiny museum of the Camargue. It is a place to linger in by oneself on a bright winter day, when there is not a tourist in the place and the whole Camargue breathes like a great organ under the rushing mistral and an oblique sun shines in a vivid blue sky. There is little to interest the æsthete or the holiday-maker, though they all have to 'do' it, and walk out hastily. There is a collection of the Camargue animals (including the almost extinct Rhône beaver), of birds (including a series of the native flamingo from nestling to adult), and not very well preserved fish from the Camargue rivers, lagoons and sea. Upstairs, among other records of the *manades*, are some relics of Baroncelli—the head of his famous bull Provence and his saddle. There is something touching about these memorials of a man who turned away from the world to live the hard life of the Camargue and foster its natural poetry.

As his name indicates, the Marquis de Baroncelli-Javon was descended from the Florentine family whose memorial chapel in Santa Croce we have all seen. He was born in 1869 at Aix-en-Provence, and as soon as he came of age abandoned 'the world' to become a *manadier*, keeping his herd on an island in the Rhône near Avignon until he moved to the Mas de l'Amarèu near the Saintes Maries, which he made a genuine life-centre until the German occupation. He was probably Mistral's favourite among the next generation of Félibres, and worked with him as assistant editor of *l'Aioli*, the Provençal periodical Mistral founded with some of the money of the Prix Reynaud. He was a person of original views and impulses. Thus, he formed a theory that the horses of the Camargue were descended from the far-off Solutrean breed, and that the gipsies were the relics of aboriginal Stone Age tribes still revisiting the shrines of their ancestors at the Saintes Maries, which was really a temple of Mithra, while 'Sara' was a priestess of the cult. Thinking his life was oppressed by evil influences, Baroncelli came to the conclusion that these could only be conjured if he sacrificed a bull to Mithra in the St. Sara crypt of the church of the Saintes Maries. He could never understand why the curé refused to authorise it.

Much more might be said in praise of Baroncelli, but he is cited here mainly because Mistral's choice of him as a close collaborator shows that whatever his personal views Mistral was determined that his Félibrige and the 'Provençal Renaissance' should not be monopolised by any religious, political or other sectarianism. It is difficult enough for a literary group to avoid that anywhere, but above all in France, where party spirit is so active and vehement. If the Félibrige was to be representative of contemporary Provence there must be room in it for all sorts. No doubt he had this as well as other objects in view when in 1884 he resigned as *Capoulié*, after thirty years, in favour of Roumanille. For him to continue as leader to the end of his life was making the Félibrige too much his personal kingdom, with the chance that after his death the whole organisation might dissolve into factions. Mistral himself was politically a very platonic Monarchist, especially after the resignation of MacMahon made the Republic a certainty; and in religion a very unfanatical Catholic. Of course, even after his resignation as *Capoulié* Mistral still remained the constitutional monarch of the Félibrige; and his determination to keep it free from dominance by his own parties is demonstrated by his supporting and securing the elections in succession as *Capoulié* of Félix Gras, a republican, and Pierre Devoluy, a Protestant.

Since we have been discussing Mistral's own religious views and shall have to touch on them again in speaking of his poem, *Nerto*, this is perhaps the moment to mention a couple of occasions on which he showed his personal independence. In 1880 the French Government decided to expel the religious orders from France, and the Premonstrant Fathers who had occupied Mistral's old abbey school of St. Michel de Frigolet received the expulsion decree like all the other abbeys and convents. They decided to put up a passive resistance and were joined by a few ardent laymen during a 'siege' of the abbey by no less than two thousand troops of the National Army. It is often stated that Mistral was one of those who stayed with the Fathers, and that like them he was eventually manhandled out of the place by the soldiers. I have before me a popular contemporary French guide-book to Provence which states this categorically as a fact; though it just is not true. It is true that the mayor of Maillane furnished the garrison with supplies, and as he was Mistral's nephew, Théophile Mistral, contemporary newspaper reports probably confused the two and so started the story. Frédéric Mistral certainly attended the mass celebrated on the last Sunday before the expulsion, and he certainly deplored and wrote at the time that he deplored this attack on liberty, adding however "it is not my affair." Above all, as A. Thibaudet remarks, it was "not the affair of the

Féllbrige." A fanciful parody of this 'siege' of St. Michel de Frigolet occurs in Daudet's *Port-Tarascon*, and he begins the chapter with affectionate references to his friend Mistral and a description of a drive with him to Tarascon—which he could not have done without being offensive to Mistral if Mistral had really been among the 'defenders' of the abbey whom Daudet ridiculed so mercilessly.

There was assuredly no obligation on any French Catholic to show a useless excess of zeal in resisting the French Army, but there is an obligation on every Catholic to ask ecclesiastical sanction for the publication of any religious work and above all any book dealing with the Bible. In the early part of this book I mentioned how Mistral spent thirty years in the production of his translation of Genesis. In his confident way Maurras assures us that Mistral translated and published in the *Armana* a chapter a year and that at the end of fifty years the work was completed. The true story is not quite so splendid as that. Mistral did publish a chapter each Christmas in the *Armana* from 1878 on, and when the book was published in 1910 some thirty chapters under various pseudonyms had appeared in it. It seems that Cardinal Cabrières, the Bishop of Montpellier, had to intervene to save him from censure, although every page had been submitted by the translator to Father Xavier de Fourvières, author of the *Pichot Tresor*. The reason usually given for his making the translation is that he thought the patriarchal life mirrored in Genesis had some similarity to that of his father's generation in Provence—and it must be remembered that the Old Testament is not read by everyone as it used to be in Protestant countries.

In spite of the continuous work of producing the *fascicules* of his dictionary, Mistral retained so much creative energy that by 1884 he was able to publish another long poem, *Nerto*, although before he had completed it his life was saddened by the death of his mother. She had lived to see her son develop from the headstrong if scatterbrained little boy, who three times in one day fell into the stream trying to get water-flowers he had been told were beyond his reach, into the poetic leader who had more influence in Provence and indeed the whole Midi than any other contemporary.

Mistral's title page describes *Nerto* as a "Provençal novel"— in verse, of course. *Mirèio* and *Calendau* are modestly described as "Provençal poems". Why the change? *Nerto* is based on an old popular legend, but it is much nearer a conventional story or even a melodrama than the earlier poems. The action passes in papal Avignon, Montmajour and Arles during the pontificate of Benedict XIII, 1394–1424; and as the characters are all in the highest rank of life the poem is in that respect far indeed from *Mirèio* and its realistic scenes of humble life in 'Rhodanie'. Perhaps that is one reason why *Nerto* is less admired or, at any rate, when mentioned is usually treated rather irrelevantly as a subject for discussing the author's orthodoxy or lack of orthodoxy. A more serious objection is that, however genuine the legend, it runs on rather fustian lines. A father who sells his daughter's soul to the devil for 'gold'. An underground passage from the papal palace of Avignon to the castle of Châteaurenard (ten kilometres off on the other side of the Durance) by which the Pope by unhistoric methods escapes from a historic siege!* A Pope's nephew, in love with the beautiful Nerte, dragging her by night forcibly from the convent in which the Pope has just placed her as a novice! The escape of Nerte to a holy hermit who proposes they shall live and pray together (inevitably recalling ribald scenes from Boccaccio), until a wise archangel gives sounder advice! Finally a scene between Devil, nun and lover in a luxurious place built by Satan's 'gramarye' in solitude, and the saving of both souls by the lover's sacrificing his carnal passion and confronting the Devil with the hilt of his sword as a cross! The disappearance of palace and all concerned in a flash of lightning and a roll of thunder, leaving nothing but a rock shaped like a kneeling nun!

Such, perhaps a little unfairly, is a rude synopsis of *Nerto*, which however flatteringly it might be reported seems a refutation of those critics who assert that Mistral was always

* The Pope did escape to Châteaurenard, but in disguise and by boat.

classic and never romantic. The trouble with *Nerto* is not so much that it is romantic, which is undeniable, as that it is operatic. What was Mistral thinking of? Was he sketching out a plan for his friend Gounod to set to music? That seems unlikely, and the truth probably is that Mistral had long known and liked the legend, and, as it was Provençal so far as he was concerned, did not care that compacts with the Devil for a soul in medieval settings were part of the Romantic stock-in-trade. What saves the whole thing from the comparative banality of the plot is the skill of execution, the amazing knowledge displayed, and the beauty of the verse. Here Mistral abandoned the stanza of his earlier narrative poems, and wisely, for only astonishing virtuosity can make the stanza a successful form for story-telling. In *Nerto* he uses a lively rhymed octosyllabic couplet, which moves quickly enough, but needs all Mistral's poetic skill to avoid monotony. It is possible that the measure was suggested to him by his studies of medieval romances in *langue d'oc* and *langue d'oïl*; which his learned friends of *Romania* were then exhuming from centuries of oblivion in old libraries.

Yet it is much more interesting both as narrative and as poem than this apparently unsympathetic analysis might suggest. The fact is that, as nearly always with Mistral, the real subject is not the ostensible one. The fate of Nerte and her lover really are less important to him than the glory of Papal Avignon and medieval Arles. For all that God, the Devil and the Pope are interested in their fates, Nerte and Rodrigue are less touching lovers than Mireille and Vincent; Petrarch's Avignon is less humanly interesting than the Mas of the Nettle-trees, but Mistral was right to show the traditional glories as well as the pastoral realities of his Rhodanie. Hardy wrote *The Dynasts* as well as *Under the Greenwood Tree*.

The verse Prologue to *Nerto* has attracted rather more attention than is due to its purely secular merits. Having decided to tell this wild Provençal legend, in which the Devil plays so important a part, Mistral naturally prepares his readers with a skilful defence of the reality of the Devil and his works, and just as naturally made it as orthodox as he could. Of course plenty of people do still believe in the Devil and his works, but the belief was obviously far less universal in 1884 than in 1404, and Mistral's instinct was sound in composing this Prologue, which is done so convincingly that some readers must unawares have found themselves saying to themselves: "Well, there may be something in it, after all." But are the views there put out with so much persuasive literary skill necessarily Mistral's? They may be, of course; but it seems unfair to an imaginative poet to attribute to him personally beliefs which are part of his theme. Nobody supposes that he believed in the existence of the "underground passages" between Avignon and Châteaurenard and between Les Baux and Cordes. He believes in the peasants' belief. Milton has never been accused of a literal belief in his hobgoblins when he:

> "Tells how the drudging Goblin sweat
> To earn his cream-bowl duly set,
> When in one night, ere glimpse of morn,
> His shadowy flail hath threshed the corn
> That ten day-labourers could not end,
> Then lies him down the lubber-fiend,
> And stretched out all the chimney's length
> Basks at the fire his hairy strength."

He may be compared with Mistral's *"Esperit-Fantasti"*, who in amiable moods "sweeps the kitchen, triples the eggs from the fowls, looks to the fire and turns the roast" but in his malice plays as many tricks as Robin Goodfellow.

Now, as we know, Mistral said he was "not religious but superstitious"; but it is unfair to build too much on a *boutade*, though of course there is other evidence. But while it is very natural to seek the poet in his writings, this kind of scrutiny may be carried too far. As Prior said:

> " 'Od's life! Must one swear to the truth of a song?"

More to the point so far as the poem *Nerto* is concerned are such brilliant passages as the long description of Avignon

166

under the Papacy. Unfortunately it is far too long to quote in full, short extracts will not give the effect, and I am already only too conscious that in trying to summarise or paraphrase Mistral I have fallen far indeed below him. Anyone who will take the trouble to read the first five or six pages of the second book of *Nerto* (*Lou Papo*) will find a brilliant evocation of papal Avignon, which is no doubt partly if not wholly historical, and whether over-idealised or not, a welcome antidote to the jeremiads of Petrarch and the not always accurate reports of our own cultured countrymen.

I have a sincere and life-long admiration for John Addington Symonds, to whose writings I owe much happiness, one who had the admirable gift of being able to place his remarkable knowledge of Greece and Italy within the comprehension of less erudite persons quite without condescension or a trace of arrogance. Excellent as Symonds's sketch of *Old Towns in Provence* may be from some points of view, he was for once rather out of the area of his scholarship, and he was too much of an invalid, a dilettante and æsthete to make any contact with the life of the Camargue, which he dismisses as "dreary" without (I suspect) having made it more than a perfunctory visit, while in his (as ever) delightful description of the view from Les Baux he paraphrases (without quotation marks) Dante's reference to Arles as the place where "the Rhône stagnates", which has ceased to be the fact since Louis XIV's engineers ill-advisedly built levees along the river. And fortunately for his admirers Symonds saves himself by the phrase "so runs tradition" (in actual fact the custodian) when he describes in the papal palace the:

". . . torture-chamber, funnel-shaped to drown and suffocate the shriek of wretches on the rack" . . .

but luckily passes over in silence the evident marks of fire in the funnel-shaped torture-chamber which the same custodian told indignant tourists showed where heretics had been burned alive. Unfortunately for this story, the "funnel-shaped" torture chamber was the papal kitchen, and no more fearful *autos-da-fé* were held there than roastings of roebuck and wild boar, of sheep and oxen, on the spit. Still, Symonds reflects, the palace has "the reek of blood in it." Perhaps it has. One never knows.

As to the endless discussions about the existence of the Devil, and whether the Baron's sale of another person's soul (even his own daughter's) was a contract valid in celestial Law, and whether *Nerto* does or does not prove that Mistral believed in the Devil and may therefore attain salvation, perhaps the best comment was unintentionally provided by the Scotch Professor of Theology who with profound gravity and emphasis told his class:

"The Devil, after succeeding in his vile machinations, retires to his infernal den and grins with horrid satisfaction."

8

Queen Jane and the Rhône

The long-drawn-out task of publishing the *Trésor*, on which work had begun as far back as 1861, was at last completed in 1885. When the moment came to bind up the *fascicules* in book form, it was found that Mistral's original estimate of 1,800 pages was too optimistic—the great work finally occupied two volumes of 1,200 pages each. Obviously, the most exacting part of the labour ended in 1874 with the completion of the actual writing of the dictionary, but the minute care and concentration needed for the proof-reading of a technical book must have been a continuous strain. It only goes to show what a sum of intellectual work may be got through by a man of Mistral's varied gifts if he has the leisure to work like Goethe "without haste but without rest."

We are so much accustomed to romantic sketches of poets as disorderly persons scribbling down a poem when they need a small subsidy to go on drinking (i.e., Verlaine), or as gentlemen of leisure composing poetry to beguile the boredom of dressing for dinner (Byron), that we forget the essential intellectual work really done by them all. Mistral made journeys to Paris, excursions with old friends, and of course his attendance was often called for to make speeches at gatherings, whether poetic or general. But when at home he must have submitted to considerable self-discipline in order to get through all the work he undertook. Unfortunately I have not been able to find any reliable account of how he arranged his working day before his marriage, but in later life his routine was something as follows:

He rose at seven after a light *café au lait* breakfast, and worked in his study until noon. These were not his best hours for creative writing, and he employed them on more prosaic work, such as proof-correcting and the heavy correspondence he had to deal with. At midday he lunched on some of the peasant Provençal dishes made for him by 'Marie', but did not take much meat, and drank only a light wine of his own making mixed with water. Much of the afternoon was devoted to study and to receiving the numerous guests, many of them strangers, who came to see him. As he often remarked smilingly but with a touch of satire, he had become part of the usual "tourist's round", ranking with Les Baux and the Roman buildings at St. Rémy as an attraction—perhaps even with one star in Baedeker. Before dinner he walked, often with his wife, at least four or five kilometres; and this was the time when his mind was active creatively and he composed the verses he wrote down after he got home. It will be remembered that Housman's inspiration was most vigorous during his afternoon walk after lunch and a sedative of a pint of beer; but we are not told if Mistral was able to compose when his wife was with him. In 1884 (if we can trust Edmond de Goncourt) he stated that "the twilight hours" out of doors were those propitious to his work as poet. He dined at seven, and was usually in bed soon after nine. Ten hours sleep seem rather a lot, but perhaps he read in bed.

When there were guests at lunch no doubt some of the more savoury Provençal dishes were served, though they are not specified; but Mistral did not then serve his ordinary wine. 'Marie' was told to bring up some bottles from the cellar, which was always well stocked since the wine-growers of the Midi, from Hermitage, Châteauneuf-du-Pape and Tavel, presented him with some of their best vintages. He liked to distinguish them when serving not by the name of the wine but by that of the giver. A pleasant glimpse, which becomes even more pleasant when we learn that 'Marie' would advise a guest what to take from a dish and, if encouraged, would give her recipes! Ajalbert rightly contrasts the patriarchal simplicity of this scene with the social pretentiousness of the average 'successful' writer of that epoch.

There is no question here of trying to give a life of Mistral but only such glimpses as may perhaps help to illustrate his work and influence. His public appearances and utterances, which I have not attempted to record, become even more numerous and extensive in the years between 1884 and 1897 when he was writing *La Rèino Jano* and his last long poem, *Lou Pouèmo dóu Rose*. His visit to Montpellier in 1878 has already been mentioned, and fortunately others are recorded, with the speeches he made. In 1879 the annual *Santo Estello* feast was held at Toulouse, and he spoke on the organisation of the Félibrige, and in 1880 a very characteristic praise of Illusion came from him—illusion as the source of all virtue and happiness, "the balm of God, the glittering mirror of youth, delight and mystery of love, and talisman of all happiness on our sad earth," which very debatable proposition he illustrated by the old Provençal story of Rudel and the Countess Mélisande of Tripoli—an apt illustration since the whole story is an invention founded on Rudel's beautiful but enigmatic poem: "*Lanquan li jorn son lonc en may . . .*" with its repeated and mysterious allusion to his "distant love, *amor de lonh*." But perhaps not so encouraging in its moral, since Rudel went to seek his mistress and found death! Mistral did himself an injustice here, for while he certainly makes constant use of imagination and legend and tradition in his work, the essential meaning of that work was the defence of the reality of an ancient way of life against the illusions of political doctrinaires, bureaucratic pedants, and machine maniacs.

At Albi in 1882 he spoke on "attachment to the soil", as usual blaming on 'centralisation' the destruction of the old life which was really the result of machine-worship, but giving as his toast the "*Vivo Toulouso!*" which was the war-cry of the Midi in its struggle against the treachery and massacre miscalled "the Albigensian Crusade". After speeches in Marseille and in Paris (both in Provençal) he spoke to the Félibres of Gap on the depopulation of the country which was going on in 1886, as it is now. It was perhaps another tribute to Illusion when he told the people of Cannes next year that the cosmopolitan idlers on the Côte d'Azur were "the lucky harbingers of the future federation of peoples."

Among his later public discourses were the reception speech to Aubanel (an excellent eulogy) on his entering the Marseille Academy in 1887; the inauguration of a monument to Roumanille at Avignon in 1904; and the brief talk of praise to the girls who had promised to wear the costume of Arles, the *Fèsto Vierginenco*. As a matter of fact the female 'costume of Arles' was comparatively recent compared with some or many of the other traditions of Rhodanie, but its dignity and attractiveness were questioned mainly by those with *modes de Paris* to sell. Mistral fought hard to save it, satirising the girls who abandoned a costume which has the grace of the Tanagra statuettes for what an indignant and eloquent ally called *"les ignominieuses saugrenuités lancées par le rastaquouèrisme de toute la planète"*! (That was in 1918.) He tried to encourage it by giving *fêtes* where no women were allowed except those wearing the costume of Arles, and the *Fèsto Vierginenco* was made the occasion for presenting a diploma, designed by Léopold Lelée, to those girls who promised to wear the dress.

These public appearances might be multiplied almost indefinitely, for like all modern monarchs Mistral was expected to countenance innumerable 'causes' and 'manifestations' if in any way linked with Provence and its language and the Félibrige. One may stand for all, the more interesting since it concerns the bull-games and ended with a distinct victory for Provence and Mistral. As far back as 1873 the Ministry of the Interior had issued an order forbidding in Provence and Languedoc both the native bull-games and the Spanish bull-fights. In making which order he was simply continuing an official war against them which had been going on at least since the reign of Louis XIV. The petition on which the Government of Louis XIV had acted sought the suppression of the bull-games (not the *mise à mort*, not then introduced into France) on the ground that a man had recently been dangerously hurt! Setting aside the occasional bruises and scratches received in the Sport of Kings, one may perhaps point to more modern sports and pastimes, including the æsthetic and muscular sport of motor-racing, in which spectators as well as participants are sometimes a little shaken.

On July 24th, 1703, an order was issued, not by the King but by the Parlement of Aix, forbidding the bull-games in the town of 'Tharascon' which still continues to have bull-games whenever it wants. Bickerings of this sort went on. In 1874 Mistral published in the *Armana* a witty 'Protest of the Bulls of the Camargue'.

Now, I personally do not like and never attend the *mise à mort* Spanish bull-fights, which to my taste too much resemble the feats of an elegant abattoir. But I cannot see any reason why they should be forbidden by a society which permits the massacre of 'pigeon shooting', fox and stag hunting, and the slaughter of grouse driven over the butts. In the Spanish type of bull-fighting, horses are ripped up, and sometimes a man is hurt or killed. I shall listen to clamours of 'brutality' when I hear of northern sportsmen gored by a pheasant or tossed by a hare.

As may easily be inferred, Mistral mainly defended the harmless Provençal bull-games, where the bull is unhurt and the skill lies in snatching a *cocarde* from his horns. But, like any other sensible man, he saw no earthly reason why the *mise à mort* should be forbidden by people who daily consumed the products of the abattoir and sometimes practised the heroic sports I have mentioned. So he backed the Midi when it decided to defy the law and give a superb bull-fight with six bulls and six toreros—double the usual number! This was held at Nîmes on October 14th, 1894, in the Roman arena, before 20,000 people. There was great applause when the mayor of Nîmes entered, accompanied by several local members of Parliament who knew which side their votes were buttered. And then came the great moment—Mistral entered, and the whole audience stood up with a great shout: "Mistral!" What is the noise of a crowd to a poet who knows he has done his best, but that the dust of time dims the loveliest poems? Yet the mutual homage was pleasant, for the crowd knew well enough that he did not like the Spanish bull-fight and had protested against the introduction of a Spanish bull strain into

173

the *manades*, so they liked him all the more for standing by them and allowing himself to be included in the summons for illegal bull-fighting. The fine, I believe, was sixteen francs, but as the good town of Nîmes or whoever it was who organised the games' made a clear profit of 50,000 (gold) francs, the fine was no serious injury.

L'Aiòli (in French spelling *l'aïoli* or *l'ailloli*), the Provençal journal which Mistral founded with the money of the Prix Jean Reynaud, was first issued on January 7th, 1891, and was continued with the assistance of Baroncelli for eight years. Incidentally, Mistral never spent on himself the money of his various literary prizes, "my poet's money" as he called it, but always gave it to help on the cause of poetry and Provence. Usually a poet's periodical is started to call attention to the writings of himself and his friends when they cannot get a hearing in other journals. But at this time Mistral was over sixty and, so far from needing the publicity of a small Provençal paper, would gladly have been relieved of some of the burdens of too much fame. He had other and less selfish motives.

Why did Mistral choose such a homely title for his new periodical? As the word itself implies, an *aiòli* is a mixture of garlic (*ai*) and olive oil (*òli*) pounded in a marble mortar to mayonnaise, and, by extension of meaning, any peasant or fisherman's meal—usually boiled vegetables and fish or even meat—to which it is a sauce. It is essentially a peasant dish of the Midi, for the amount of garlic in it (at least two whole cloves pounded to pulp) would horrify the bourgeois world anywhere. It was an excellent title for his purpose, which was to regain touch with the people. Mistral must have realised that, while in the 1850s and 1860s the annual Almanac sufficed, this was hardly the case in the 1890s when a new generation had arisen, educated in schools where French was obligatory and the children punished for speaking *patois*, while several French periodicals were aimed at them. At any rate in his introduction to the first number of *L'Aiòli* he says that he means by it a "stirring up of Provençal affairs in our own language." Continuing the metaphor, he hopes his '*aiòli*' will be eaten (one might here aptly use the Victorian 'discussed') in the fields, the cottages, the little farms. He makes his mayonnaise a symbol of union—of the different provinces of the Midi! For he goes on to denounce that "northern frost", the "Franchiman's arrogance" which was killing the old, free and easy spirit of Provence.

What success *L'Aiòli* had in gaining readers "in the fields and farms" is nowhere stated, though the dropping of the paper in 1898 seems to indicate a lack of the success which the Almanac achieved, seeing that it started in 1854 and still goes on. True, *L'Aiòli* was particularly Mistral's own mouthpiece rather than that of the Félibrige. And then in 1898 he was sixty eight and absorbed in his work for the Museon Arlaten, though if the paper had really succeeded one would think Mistral would have preferred to hand it over to Baroncelli and other young men rather than let it die. His 'Nostradamus' whim of bringing it out on the 7th, 17th, and 27th of each month may not have suited his readers as well as it suited him. Mistral's own contributions to *L'Aiòli* do not differ in any essentials from those he had contributed for so many years and continued to contribute to the Almanac.

One of the best is the brief farewell notice he wrote at the end of 1896 on hearing of the death of Paul Arène. Among the writers of the Mistral epoch who wrote in French on themes of Provence three are still widely read—Jean Aicard, Alphonse Daudet and Paul Arène. Aicard is the least distinguished of the three, and the highbrows won't hear of him; but *Maurin des Maures* and its successor have their place and are particularly pleasing to the young in reading who look for enjoyment rather than for perfection.

Daudet was Mistral's old and familiar friend and as such regarded by the Maître with warm affection. The *Tartarin* and *Moulin* books are so accessible that they are likely to be the first read by those exploring the books and life and places of the Midi. The first *Tartarin* and some of the short stories are as fresh and amusing now as when they were published nearly a century ago. But one comes to see that Daudet was a bit of a *faux frère*, exploiting the Midi for the amusement of the Parisians and very careful always to keep on the right side of his public. Mistral of course knew this perfectly well, but his affection for Daudet was too solid to be destroyed, and then—such is human nature!—Daudet's immense popular reputation was far too valuable to the 'cause' to be rejected. Still, let us recognise it—though the first *Tartarin* is a caricature it is often very funny, while the two successors are more of a caricature and too seldom funny. Far better are the pick of the *Moulin* stories, but there is a touch of the factitious even about them. Daudet never lived in his mill which he describes so 'poetically' but in a large comfortable house belonging to friends in Fontvieille, while in any case most of these stories were written in Paris.

No, we all begin with Daudet and hold on gladly to the best in him, but in the end we prefer Paul Arène. The comparison is unfair in a way, since he was mainly a writer of short stories, but as an interpreter of the life and lands of the Midi he is less vivid and attractive than our contemporaries Maurice Chauvet of Languedoc and Marie Mauron of Provence. Quite apart from his *Chèvre d'Or*—where would the Provençal writers be without that famous golden goat who watches over the hidden treasures for them?—his short stories are more delicate and finely observed than Daudet's though they lack his Dickensian verve and humour. Mistral was right to praise and to regret Paul Arène. Nothing matters to the dead, yet it seems the last irony of a rather sad life that Arène did not even get the epitaph he told Mistral he had chosen for himself, which was: *Gaio, ai pantaia ma vido*—gay I dreamed my life. Whereas what they put over him was: "I go, my soul in delight at having dreamed my life." He was born in Sisteron, and after living much of his life in Paris (where he helped to found the Félibrige of Paris at the Café Voltaire) he died at Antibes and was buried in his native place, which he described so beautifully yet sadly as the half-deserted Canteperdrix.

However, so far as Mistral's contributions to *L'Aiòli* are concerned, the article on Paul Arène was exceptional and an act of homage to a recently dead literary comrade, for in general his articles are more 'popular' in subject, though he does discuss the question of a Provençal University, and of course there are the inevitable discussions about the two languages. On the whole, then, it seems fair to say that *L'Aiòli* was a bid to regain direct touch with the 'people' as a writer, which Mistral had been in some danger of losing since *Mirèio*, mainly because of his twenty years absorption in the task of producing his dictionary. Of course, his prestige and popularity as the great figure of contemporary Provence had never stopped growing—he had unquestionably more influence in the Midi than any living person.

Although the themes of *Calendau* and *Nerto* were based on popular legends, the poems themselves were not 'popular' in the sense that *Mirèio* and *Magali* and even the *Coupo Santo* were. In spite of Charles Maurras's pedantic and dogmatic assertions that Mistral was wholly 'classic', the obvious fact is that both *Calendau* and *Nerto* are nearly related to French Romanticism. Tennyson knew Virgil as thoroughly as Mistral did, but *Maud* is no more 'classic'—and no less—than *Mirèio*. Of course, the legends of *Nerto* and those brought into *Calendau* are part of the 'tradition of Provence' as preserved in the farms and fields and workshops. But the treatment and workmanship are not 'traditional Provençal'. An *image d'Epinal* and a Salon picture may both treat the same subject—but how differently!

It is a question whether Mistral's next important publication, *La Rèino Jano* (1890), was also intended as a means of re-establishing contact with the 'people'. So far as I know, Mistral made no statement on the subject, but obviously successful plays are an excellent means of popularising a movement like the Félibrige, even if they don't get to the small farms and the people working in the fields. A good beginning had been made by the amiable Théodore Aubanel, whose *Lou Pan dòu Pecat* (The Bread of Sin) had been produced in Provençal at Montpellier, while a French translation by Paul Arène achieved the honour of production at the Odéon. Aubanel wrote another play, *Lou Pastre* (The Shepherd), in rather peculiar circumstances. In 1865 the poet had to serve on the jury at Carpentras, where one of the cases was a rather grim and tragical story of rape. In contrast to his own cheerful and innocent life at Avignon this revelation of life at a different level seems to have impressed Aubanel greatly; but he was wise enough not to show the resulting play, since he realised that charitable criticism would probably accuse him of drawing on his own experience for facts he had merely heard *in camera* at the court of Carpentras. I believe the original text never has been published, though a revised version was published after the poet's death.

Mistral may well have thought that a tragedy might be built on loftier ground than rape and the bread of sin, and in choosing as his subject the life of Joanna the First of Naples and Provence he was certainly taking a legend created by the 'people'. I have already pointed out, I hope not too pedantically, that Mistral overstepped the limits of art and history when he tried to prove that the legendary Joanna is the real one. Of course the fragmentary and contradictory notices surviving about a person, even a queen, who lived so long ago as the fourteenth century leave plenty of room for conjectures. Like Mary Stuart, whose fate in some ways resembled hers, Joanna was born to the difficult and dangerous task of a queen regnant, with rather more of the woman than the ruler in her. Whatever history says, the artists can make as many interpretations of her as they have of Mary Stuart. Among Mistral's predecessors was Walter Savage Landor, who has left a play about Joanna as the central part of a not very playable trilogy. In that respect Mistral has hardly been more successful. The praises of Provence in the first act are too long-drawn-out and like all such partialities become wearisome; the murder of the King, Andrew of Hungary, is unconvincing; there are too many lyrics, especially during the sea voyage from Naples to Marseille; and the triumphant and flattering reception of Joanna in Provence too fantastically improbable. In fact, she was a fugitive from her kingdom of Naples because it was invaded by the angry countrymen of her murdered husband.

178

She stayed only a short time in Provence, where her main transaction was the selling of Avignon and the Comté Venaisson to the shrewd Clement VI for a quite inadequate sum (which, it is said, was never paid) in order to be cleared of the fearful charge hanging over her. Her other services to Provence consisted in taking its ships, money and nobles for the re-conquest of Naples, and in appointing an Italian as her viceroy!

Just how it was that the popular imagination made Joanna into the ideal and beloved monarch, and indeed the only one remembered, is a question which would have tempted Sir Thomas Browne. Leaving out the influence of "tutelary observators", we may reasonably suppose that to the people of Provence Joanna was the symbol of the native rulers they wished they had had in the days before the King of France became Comte de Provence. It is said that she became confused with the wholly mythical Pope Joan and with the Joanna who was wife of "le bon Roi René"—another Provençal character whose active benevolence seems rather imaginary, unless indeed he did introduce muscat grapes to Provence. But he was a sort of early Renaissance John Lackland, always stoutly boasting that he would not preside over the liquidation of his kingdom, and meekly giving up a province every few months. No wonder the Provençaux preferred Joanna of Naples. Unluckily, the general opinion seems to be that Mistral not only failed to make an actable play out of her life, but that his poem in dramatic form is not among his successes. I don't presume to set my opinion against those of Jules Lemaître and A. Thibaudet, but I must say that I think they and other critics have passed harsh judgment on La Rèino Jano because it is not good Parisian theatre, and failed altogether to consider it as poetry. Our Brownings and Swinburnes, Tennysons and Eliots have accustomed us to admire poems in dramatic form, in spite of the notorious fact that they do not reach the stage standards of Noël Coward and Shakespeare.

A pleasing aspect of this affair is that Mistral wrote about Naples first, and visited it afterwards. The letters written by

Mistral during his trip to Italy in the spring of 1891 were published in *L'Aiòli* and later translated into French by Charles Maurras. Perhaps the most interesting person he met was Carducci, and the prettiest little anecdote is of the Italian Customs officer who instead of tumbling over all the contents of the Mistral's baggage gravely saluted when showed the diploma appointing Mistral an Officer of the Corona d'Italia on the occasion of the Petrarch centenary celebrations at Avignon. Other passages in which Rome (for instance) is compared unfavourably with the Roman remains of Provence are less happy, and suggests that there is a point where even the best-founded and most agreeable regionalism becomes provincialism. And it is stretching a point to state that Santa Chiara in Naples was "built by la Reine Jeanne," considering that it was begun by her grandfather Robert, nearly twenty years before she was born. Another curious little point accidentally revealed by these letters from Italy is that—as more than one of his personal friends state—Mistral in spite of his dignified and even imposing appearance was actually not only modest but rather timid.

Apropos the over-valuing of objects simply because they were Provençal, this seems the moment to say a word about the Venus of Arles (now in the Louvre), which it was an article of Félibrige faith to consider as one of the finest works of ancient Greek art. The statue was found broken in a well during some excavations of the theatre at Arles in 1651; and in 1683 was unwisely given by the city to Louis XIV, who set it up at Versailles after it had been over-restored in the taste of the time by Girardon. Somewhere about 1911, there was a threat to deprive Arles of a cast of the statue made before Girardon had meddled with it. A comparison of photographs shows that the disaster of the restoration was worse even than one might have feared—there is nothing much Greek remaining except the marble itself. It is recorded that Mistral was hesitant and even rather shocked by these revelations. They disturbed the traditional belief in the glories of the Venus of Arles, though he might have reminded himself that there is more humbug than truth about much 'good taste' in the fine arts

Whatever doubts and reserves have to be made about *Nerto* and *La Rèino Jano*, there can be no doubt that Mistral achieved one of his most admired successes in 1897 with his last long poem, *Lou Pouèmo dóu Rose*. Here he abandoned quasi-historical or legendary medievalism and returned to the people and epoch which best inspired him. It is the poem of the river from Lyon to Beaucaire, but above all of the Rhône sailors, the last generation of those who from pre-Greek and even pre-Celtic times had made the river one of the great commercial highways of Europe. The supernatural element (apart from one unimportant episode) is appropriate, even though the main action (like that of *Mirèio*) is natural and realistic and set in the beginning of the nineteenth century—a period about which Mistral as a child and youth heard so many tales and reminiscences and legends from survivors. The patriarchal agricultural life so vividly portrayed in *Mirèio* changed and in the end was profoundly modified by economic, social and mechanical forces, but it went on, and much more survived than might be supposed. The age-old life and labour of the Rhône sailors was rapidly and completely abolished, mainly by the building of the railways but also by the application of steam to the Rhône navigation.

The towns just above the Rhône delta—Arles, Tarascon, Beaucaire, Avignon—were long the natural centres of a considerable *entrepôt* trade. Inland products, floated rapidly down the Rhône in *sicelandes* and *sapines* from Lyon and other river towns, were transferred, particularly at Arles, to small sea-going vessels which had brought salt and other Mediterranean goods. The main difficulty of course was the passage up a swift river, with islands, rocks, sand-banks which shifted, sudden floods, so that some of the scenes described by Mistral might almost have come from Mark Twain's *Life on the Mississippi*. The pre-steam train of Rhône barges was slowly dragged up-stream by teams of twenty to forty horses arranged by fours, and took about a month from Arles to Lyon. In 1828 the first steam paddle-boat made the same voyage with a cargo of over 100 tons in about two days. By the time the railway was finished in 1848, the age-old horse and barge type of navigation was gone for ever. Yet the steam-boats themselves were soon displaced by tugs and they in turn by the motor-barge. The net result is that the immense animation of the old river traffic, which gave employment to thousands and developed such curious types of boat, has almost disappeared. One does occasionally see a barge on the Grand Rhône or two or three tied up at Arles, but a mere shadow of what was, while the Petit Rhône seems never to be used at all—in years I have never seen anything on it but the ferry and an occasional fisherman's punt. Yet Route Nationale number 7, which runs parallel to the Rhône, is a perpetual nightmare of roaring lorries and certainly the most dangerous road in France. *On sent le progrès.* Let us hope that the long-promised opening of the river to barges of 1,200 tons will some day come true.

The main theme of the Rhône poem is the evocation of that lost life and its sudden destruction, symbolised in the poem by the sinking of the barge train and the drowning of its magnificent team of horses through collision with a descending paddle-boat. Patron Apian, owner and skipper, refuses to make way for the smoke-belching monster—"the Rhône is ours"—and pays the penalty of opposition to Progress. Threaded through this tragical story is the legend, full of typically Provençal supernatural details, of the love of Anglore and the "little Prince of Orange" who is also a Rhône Drac. 'Anglore' is the nickname of the eldest girl of a Rhône pilot, who lives with her mother and brothers and sisters near the junction of the Ardèche and the Rhône, and makes pocket-money by washing out the gold dust from the sands brought down by the Ardèche. *Anglore* means a lizard, and the name was given to the girl because she was always out in the sun. . . .

And then she fell in love with the Drac. What is a Drac? In the first place, he or it must not be confused with the Tarasque, which, as everyone knows, has six legs, a formidable tail, an underbody covered with scales, a carapace which looks

like that of a gigantic armadillo with spikes and a stylised back
ridge, and a terrifying face—something between a horned
Saracen and a huge cat—which when not chumping up a
Christian with his legs sticking out of its mouth is sneezing fire-
works to terrify and charm the children. This amiable
monster, which Clemenceau was so anxious to abolish, may
perhaps belong to the genus Drac, but it is a speciality of
Tarascon, and in any case not *the* Drac of Anglore and the
Rhône poem.

For the official description of Anglore's Prince of Orange
Drac we have to go to Mistral:

> " . . . Superbe,
> Anguiela coume un lampre, se bidorso
> Dins l'embut di revòu mounte blanquejo
> Emé si dous iue glas que vous trafuron.
> A lou pèu long, verdau, flus coume d'augo,
> Que floto sus sa tèsto au brand de l'oundo.
> A li det, lis artèu, pèr ausi dire,
> Tela couma un flamen de la Camargo
> E dos alo de pèis darriè l'esquino
> Clareto coume dos dentello bluio."

(Splendid and slim as a lamprey, he twists in the water-
whorls, and his green eyes seem to pierce you from his white-
ness. His long green hair, silky as sea-weed, undulates from his
head in the waves. His fingers and toes, they say, are webbed
like a flamingo in the Camargue, and there are two fins at his
back as transparent as blue lace.)

A habit of the Drac was to decoy women to his underwater den, as happened to a washerwoman who dropped her
wooden clothes-beater in the river and in trying to recover it
found herself dragged down and condemned for seven years to
look after a child the Drac had had by a half-drowned girl.
Anglore herself had seen and almost yielded to the Drac one
hot summer night when bathing, but in the end he slipped

away leaving a flowering rush as a token. The Drac can take any form he wants, so that when the young Prince of Orange meets her on the barge descending the river and she looks into his green eyes while he offers her a flowering rush, she recognises her Drac at once. A prince! What girl would fail to recognise in him her mysterious water-lover?

Unluckily, as in nearly all Mistral's love stories, the end of this one was tragedy. In the disastrous collision between the paddle-steamer and Patron Apian's train of barges, the lovers are hurled into the Rhône by the shock, and never seen again. Now, why did he make that ending (no one else is drowned), when it would have been perfectly easy to send the lovers off to live happy ever after in Holland? The mystery is increased by the fact that we do not really find out whether the "Prince of Orange" is a mortal man or the Drac in one of his disguises, and so never know whether Anglore is unhappily drowned or whether she is taken by the Drac to live in his underwater den or cave, like the washerwoman who nursed his child for seven years. Obviously Mistral intentionally left it vague, which is the most effective method of using the supernatural. We can believe as much or as little as we choose, or take it as merely symbolical of the river's destructive power. Symbolical also no doubt are the allusions to Mithra, who seems to be in some ways indentified with the Drac. But the real theme of the poem is the Rhône and its sailors, just as the theme of *Mirèio* is Rhodanie and its peasants.

The Rhône poem is undoubtedly the finest example of Mistral's art as a narrative poet, even though it lacks the detailed realism and intimacy which have kept *Mirèio* always the popular favourite. What may be regretted in the earlier poems is not the 'folk-lore' (of which there is just as much in the Rhône poem) but the use of the rhymed stanza, which even in the most skilful hands tends to diffusion and digression. *Nerto* improved on this, but the rhymed octosyllables become monotonous in time. The Rhône poem is constructed in short sections (well over a hundred) or *laisses* of unrhymed eleven-syllable verses of which the last is mute. Even assonance is avoided, so that to an English-speaking reader—who, of course, cannot expect to feel the rhythm and music as a native does—the effect is that of excellent and swiftly-moving blank verse. But these are questions for metrists. The Rhône poem itself is certainly one of the most original productions of its time, and yet the inevitable complement to Mistral's other great narratives of Provence.

9

Museon Arlaten

Ordinarily the life of a man, even of a poet, between sixty-five and eighty-three, is marked by a decline of energy and a tendency to seek retirement and repose. Such is not the case with Mistral, even as a writer, while his influence and prestige as *the* public figure of the Midi increased, and his energy created what has proved to be one of the most enduring and valuable monuments, the Museon Arlaten. True, the translation of Genesis was a mere side-task for a man of his vigour and genius, while even the collection of short poems, *Lis Oulivado*, is rather a continuation of his earlier work than a new departure. *Lis Oulivado*, published in 1912, when the poet was over eighty, is his farewell book. The title, which might be rendered 'The Olive-gathering', is an allusion to the fact that in Provence the last crop of the year is the olive-gathering, and the dedication runs thus:

> "Lou tèms que se refrejo e la mar que salivo,
> Tout me dis que l'ivèr es arriba pèr iéu,
> E que fau, lèu e lèu, acampa mis òulivo
> E n'òufri l'òli vierge a l'autar dòu bon Diéu."

(The weather has turned cold and the sea is rough—everything warns me that for me winter is here and I must gather my olives now to offer the first oil to God.)

The sadness of that needs no stressing, but the same epoch saw the publication of *Moun Espelido*, a European classic, one of the most fascinating autobiographies ever published, whose only fault is that it did not go on longer. The earlier part of

186

this book owes so much to it that nothing more need be said except to stress the fact that there is no available English translation, though one would think it would be a standard book. It is a much more wholesome book than Cellini's memoirs and Rousseau's confessions.

Those last years were a season of anniversaries and of honours. In 1904 the fiftieth anniversary of the founding of the Félibrige was celebrated at Font-Ségugne. There must have been a certain melancholy for Mistral in these festivities, when among other distinctions he was given a small barrel of Tavel of the year 1870, a great vintage year, for of the other six founders of the Sainte-Estelle all were dead except Mathieu and Tavan. Of course there were new friends, and a new generation of Félibres, while the 'movement' itself had gone beyond the highest hopes of the original seven. The song he wrote for the occasion did not forget them ("The singers are dead, but their voices re-echo; the builders are dead, but the temple is built"), but even that must have reminded him of the gayer song which celebrated the first Font-Ségugne: "We are brothers and friends . . . we are the Félibres, the gay Félibres of Provence"!

May 29th, 30th and 31st, 1909, produced a series of fêtes and rejoicings for the fiftieth anniversary of the publication of *Mirèio* such as very few poets have received in their lifetime. It is true that excess of zeal among his admirers led to the disorders of the gathering at Saint Gilles and above all to the bronze statue in Arles which, as we have already seen, the poet complained was a "brick dropped on his head", while he told the sculptor (Charles Roux): "I shan't dare to walk about Arles any more. People will say: 'Hullo, here's the bronze come off its pedestal!'" However, when the dire moment arrived, and the poet standing by his statue had to return thanks for all the compliments paid him, he merely said:

"By way of thanks for all the kind things which have just been said of me, I can't do anything better than to say:
"*'Cante uno chato de Prouvenço . . .!'*"

and recited the opening stanzas of his poem. Since that was what they were celebrating, it was surely an elegant solution of a most difficult situation and of the problem: What to say when returning thanks for the unveiling of your own statue?*

There were other celebrations more to his taste—songs and *farandoles* and a ball where all the girls wore the Arles costume. The culmination came at the performance of Gounod's *Mireille* in the arena of Arles. A painting by José Belon, preserved in the Museon Arlaten, shows the crowded audience of thousands of men and women of Provence rising to greet the poet as he entered to take his seat. Among those who before him had received the acclamations of the crowd in the same amphitheatre were the Emperors Gallus and Volusianus, Constantine I, Constantius II and Majorianus, if tradition may be believed.

In 1901 the first Nobel Literary Prize was awarded to Sully-Prudhomme (who succumbed under the weight of the honour), while the German philologists and Mistral's friends actively pressed his claims. Indeed a false rumour appeared in the newspapers that it had gone to Mistral, with the result, as he humorously wrote his friends, that in a few days he had urgent requests for loans and contributions amounting to 150,000 gold francs! What a pity the Swedish Academy does not adopt the wise rules of the French National Lottery, where the winner of the *gros lot* is able to remain anonymous and so selfishly enjoy his winnings without the impertinence of paupers' letters.

And then, in 1904, the Nobel Literary Prize was divided between Mistral and the Spanish popular playwriter, José Echegaray y Eizaguirre, who at one time had been Spanish Minister of Education and then of Finance at Madrid. Why Mistral's prize had to be divided with this not very important author has never been made clear, but doubtless it was simply

---

* The statue of Mireille at the Saintes Maries de la Mer was not put up until September 1920, in the presence of Madame Mistral. The sculptor was Antonin Mercie.

another one of those *guffes* which statesmen call 'compromises'. Very little indeed is said about Echegaray's share in this award, which would have been understandable if he had been a Catalan, but he wasn't. The 'explanation' put out by one of Mistral's adherents is that the Swedish Academy did not fully appreciate Mistral because they could not read Provençal and, as Mistral did not know Swedish, the Swedish translation was unworthy of the original. This seems a little disingenuous, for the Swedish Academy could certainly read English, German and French. There was a quite adequate English translation by Harriet Preston; the German translation was excellent; and the French translation was made by Mistral himself. Nobel wished his literary prize to go to a young man of idealistic views (someone like Shelley) who was poor and needed publicity; so obviously the right 'compromise' was to split it between two well-known septuagenarians who didn't need the money. Thus, Mistral came to receive an award of 100,000 gold francs; and made a better use of the money than is sometimes the case —Anatole France gave his Nobel Prize to the Bolshevists.

Which of course brings us to the Museon Arlaten, the great work of Mistral's old age, and one of his four magnificent achievements—the other three being his life, his poetry, and the Félibrige, under which I include the *Trésor*. Before going on to the Museon we may refer again to the fact that this Nobel half-prize and the ensuing newspaper publicity seem to have revealed Mistral to the English-speaking world. True, there had been English translations, and Downer's book on Mistral was published in New York in 1901, but it is fair to say that before 1904 not much was written about contemporary Provence, and Mistral was almost always ignored, whereas after 1904 there are a number of English travel books (most of them very good in one way or another), and Mistral is invariably mentioned at length, visited during his lifetime, and his writings are quoted. The more refined type of pre-1914 æsthete evidently found Provence comparatively unattractive and uncivilised. Arthur Symons was an exception, though he did speak of Mistral's "quaint simplicity"(!) and "perilous closeness to nature"(!), but J. A. Symonds for once is superficial and inaccurate and does not mention Mistral, while Henry James, who advises the visitor to see the walls of Carcassonne from a carriage, reported that the rough paving of Arles hurt his feet and the hotel was uncomfortable. The Rev. S. Baring-Gould, a more robust traveller, saw a great deal in a short time and evidently made friends with all conditions of men, yet (writing in 1890) does not mention Mistral or the Félibrige. One would suppose that a scholar like Baring-Gould would have noticed the Mistral books in Roumanille's shop window, as Bonaparte-Wyse had done so many years earlier. But these 'classics' are sometimes rather indifferent to modern languages, and Baring-Gould passes off some very fancy French (which cannot all be put down to misprints and pen-slips) and describes *Aucassin et Nicolette* as Provençal, when it is certainly written in a north French dialect, and the author had never even seen the Beaucaire he writes about.

Obviously there must have been others beside Arthur Symons. Although Sir Theodore Cook's excellent book, *Old Provence*, was not published until 1905, his knowledge of Mistral personally and of his works could hardly have been worked up *ad hoc* after the announcement of the award, especially since he says:

"The magnificent Provençal dictionary, in which Mistral enshrined the language he has done so much to make immortal, is the best proof that his poems are a true and sincere reflection of his people and his own country."

It would not be fair to blame England for the remarks of Francis Hueffer (Dr. Franz Hüffer), a distinguished and cultured German who was naturalised English and was the father of Ford Madox Ford. His book on the medieval troubadours was published in England in 1878, and must have been something of a pioneer book there. His remarks on Mistral do not imply much first-hand knowledge of the subject and may perhaps reflect the scornful views of German philologists before the publication of the *Trésor* revealed a new language for them to prey on:

"The *patois* of Mistral's *Mireïo* (sic) has little in common with the language of the mediæval singers, and his gifted disciples' strenuous efforts stand little chance against the crushing influence of an idiom formed by Voltaire's prose and Alfred de Musset's poetry."

It is interesting to find a similarly ill-founded pessimism in Thomas Okey's otherwise well-informed and pleasant book on Avignon:

"The movement . . . has, probably, little future. Provençal is fast disappearing as a spoken language, and lingers only in a few remote villages" [such as Avignon!]; "even the master, Mistral's works are published in French as well as in Provençal. . . . The poems of Mistral and his fellow félibres are the swan-song of a dying tongue."

In the fifty years following the Font-Ségugne meeting it is estimated that some five thousand works were published in *langue d'oc* or Provençal; and in spite of the two destructive wars the production has not flagged. I can only repeat what I have said earlier—that in the very city Okey's book describes I myself heard the Archbishop preach in the cathedral in Provençal to an overcrowded congregation, lunched with at least three hundred other Félibres (all of whom but myself spoke the *langue d'oc* from Barcelona to Nice), and listened to many Provençal speakers, including the suffragan Bishop and a former Prime Minister of France! Now why do these foreign writers want to belittle a 'movement' of which they cannot have known much, since years are needed for a foreigner to become even a beginner in a very difficult language and an extensive literature? The answer is long and would not be complimentary. Contrast those writers with Roy Campbell, a great poet and the only English-speaking man who has really lived the life of Provence, as a Martigues fisherman and as a *Razeteur* of great fame who cut the *cocardes* from innumerable bulls. I won't quote his admirable autobiography, which everyone must read entire, but a single sentence from the Preface to the 1950 edition of *Adamastor*:

> "Several of the best of these poems are almost para-phrases, notably the *Horses on the Camargue* which was 'lifted' from the great Provençal poet, Mistral, who has had a powerful influence on my later work published after *Adamastor*."

In the list of members of the committee which organised the festival for the fiftieth anniversary of *Mirèio*, no Americans or British names are included. France was represented by Paul Meyer, Antoine Thomas and the Aix professor, Léopold Constans; Germany by Appel, Foerster, Morf, Stengel, Tobler and Volmöller; Italy by De Lellis, Crescini and Novatis; Luxembourg by Welter; Austria by Cornu; Holland by Salverda de Grave; Sweden by Wahlund; and Portugal by Leite de Vasconcellos. Now, most of these people were professors and philologists, not poets; so that the rejoicings seem to have been devised less in honour of the poet of *Mirèio* than of the restorer of the *langue d'oc*. Doubtless this means no more than that, as usually happens in such affairs, the committee got into the hands of a clique. Yet it does seem as if foreign countries tended to admire Mistral mainly as the compiler of the *Trésor*. It is a fact that, among the honorary degrees he received, that given by the University of Halle specified that it was given for his knowledge of the Provençal language. Possibly this meant more to Mistral even than recognition as a poet. Whether England or the United States could at that time show any distinguished 'Romanistes' I don't know.

Gaston Paris wrote of Mistral that although like every other artist he enjoyed his fame he would gladly have sacrificed his personal reputation to secure the triumph of the 'Idea' to

which he had devoted his life—Provence. That was true, and
in no mere fanatical 'my-country-right-or-wrong' sense—he
was working to save a civilisation, not to impose power. And
as it happens that a man sacrifices everything for personal
renown, and doesn't get it; so Mistral, who worked for aims
beyond himself personally, not only achieved them, but had
added unto him lasting fame among his own people. As it
has turned out, the Museon Arlaten has proved to be a more
effective monument to Mistral than many statues, though he
designed it for the glory of Arles and Rhodanie, and not of
himself.

The project was first announced by Mistral in 1896, in No.
182 of L'Aiòli. He begins by saying that Arles has two
museums (at that time, for others have been added since), the
Musée Réattu with its pictures, and the Musée Lapidaire with
its sculpture and architectural fragments and inscriptions. But,
he says, the Museon Arlaten has yet to be founded, "the true
museum of the living life and people of Arles". That is what
differentiates it from other museums, though of course it has
since had many imitators. It was not to be a collection of works
of art or antiquities (however beautiful and important for
general culture) but the record of the life and habits of a
people; and after the windfall of the Nobel Prize he was able
to enlarge it as the 'Palace of the Félibrige'. Naturally the
passage of sixty destructive years and the increasing worship of
machines and machine-products as ends not means have made
into relics of the past what was then still a part of daily life.
Mistral realised the danger because later in the same article he
says he wants to bring together all the utensils and objects of a
Mas "before the ignorance of pretended progress has wiped
them out". And he goes on to enumerate: the pots, the
narrow-necked jugs, the oil jars, the water-pots, the earthen-
ware skillets, the large wine-pots with handles, the harvesters'
dish, and so on, and a hundred other objects from the women's
costume to the equipment of a shepherd.

This first and modest collection was housed in the Arles
Chamber of Commerce, but with the Nobel money Mistral

was enabled to buy (after infinite difficulties which were eventually smoothed away by Briand) what was then the Jesuit College, part of it the ancient town mansion of the Castellane family. The courtyard, as you enter from the street, has been excavated to show Roman buildings buried and forgotten for many centuries, as they must be under most of Arles. The one poor compensation for the bombing which destroyed the old Trinquetaille quarter is that the sites and ground plans of Roman buildings were revealed. When you see what has been built since, you almost regret that the ruins weren't left.

The present greatly enlarged collection, which has been added to since his death by relics of Mistral, is an admirable commentary on his writings. It has the advantage of not being too big—just about thirty rooms and corridors—and above all of being a unity. Of course it must not be compared with the great national collections of art and antiquities of all epochs— Louvre, Metropolitan, British Museum—which are illustrative of empires and aristocracies rather than of 'common' peoples and are confusingly miscellaneous at that. Mistral limited himself to his Rhodanie and mostly though not wholly to the people and their lives.

Thus, at the very entrance, if you don't allow yourself to be distracted by the very fine example of coloured tile flooring, you will find the walls hung with dried plants from a herbal collected by Alfred Mistral. Not very thrilling to non-botanists, but Mistral has taken the trouble to write by each its Provençal name and a note on the supposed medicinal or magical properties invented for them by the prolific imagination of the Midi. All the familiar plants are there, of course, including the fragrant thyme and rosemary of the hills, but the most curious is the mandrake (Shakespeare's mandragora), also known as 'the hand of glory', which had the strange and valuable power of bewitching anyone its owner wished, and at the same time doubling his money every day. Without a suspicion of a smile the modern Provençaux will tell you: "Of course our peasants don't believe that any more—Progress, you know, Progress—but there's still a considerable sale for the roots in Cannes, Nice and Monte Carlo."

The stairway leading to the main galleries is decorated with a wrought-iron design of the 'Coupo Santo' and the *pervenche*, which is the emblematic flower of the Félibrige, while the walls are hung with banners of the ancient Guilds suppressed at the first Revolution. Three large rooms are given up to the 'costume of Arles', chiefly of course the women's, though the men's is also represented. It dates only from Louis XV (a period of prosperity in Provence, it seems) and evolved with the changing fashions until Mistral, to prevent its disappearance under the deluge of machine-stuff, decreed that it should remain as in 1904.

This leads naturally to the furniture, and then we come to one of the most interesting rooms, which illustrates myth, religion and superstition. Here are illustrations of the Saintes Maries and St. Gens, St. Martha and the Tarasque, dominated for some reason by a sinister red *bonnet phrygien* of the Revolution. There is a case of *santons*, the brightly-coloured terra-cotta little figures for the Christmas *crèches*, still sold at street corners and in little shops at Christmas time. (They are recent—eighteenth–nineteenth century in origin.) There is an immense display of amulets, but I have never been able to find the lock of golden hair from the tomb of some "dear dead woman" of Les Baux which is supposed to be there. Perhaps a wise piety has removed it. Then there are reminders of the dances and games, pilgrim medals, and the shaped breads and cakes in honour of various saints.

Another stone stairway—with souvenirs of Alphonse Daudet and his long friendship with Mistral. The next room is more like the conventional museum, since it is devoted to the history of the kingdom of Arles, from Greek coins to medieval seals and books in Provençal before the Revolution. In the rooms of paintings which follow, the most interesting are the numerous drawings of Arlésiennes by Léo Lelée and Belon's 'documentary' of Mistral at the Mireille celebrations. I can see why we are given Ziem as the painter of Martigues, and even reproductions of the overrated van Gogh; but how explain the absence of a much greater painter, who was born at Aix, and added lustre even to Provence—Cézanne? There are religious pictures and romantic art illustrating the Arles of 1850 and *Mirèio*.

Although the next galleries begin with a penny-farthing bicycle (which always reminds me of the one which used to be displayed on Sunset Boulevard, Hollywood), they are among the most interesting of the whole exhibition and repay very close inspection, since they are devoted to the arts and crafts of the area, iron-work, tools of all sorts, *micocoulier* pitchforks, basket work from the osiers of Vallabrégues (the home of Vincent and his father), dyes, silk- and wool-raising, the almond, vine and olive, the various types of mill. *Mirèio* is illustrated every moment, as the next hall, devoted to the Rhône and the Mediterranean, illustrate *Calendau* and the *Pouèmo dóu Rose*; and then we come back to *Mirèio* with the most interesting exhibits of the Crau and the Camargue. There are even old decrees regulating the *transhumance* of the sheep to and from the Alps, and maps of the *drailles*. Curious, how little one part of the world knows of another. Although this annual migration of sheep is at least as widespread in southern Italy as in Provence and of course is of immense antiquity, an Australian friend writes me the Gippsland sheep-farmers refuse to believe such a thing can happen! Which reminds me of another Australian friend who got hopelessly involved with Devon shepherds—he asking them how many acres to the sheep, and they were talking about how many sheep to the acre!

The two next rooms are reconstructions of scenes already described in these pages—the visit to the young mother, and the Christmas Eve celebrations, carried out with wax figures and the correct furnishing. In the first, as I have said, the'young mother lies in bed with her child, and the women visitors in their best dresses bring the child an egg, a roll of bread, salt and a long match-stick.

I have already described the next scene, the Christmas Eve celebrations at the Mas which made so lasting an impression

on Mistral's mind. Among other reasons for studying the
Museon reconstruction carefully is that the old man who is
dripping wine on the Yule log must have been modelled after
Mistral's father, while it is said that the younger man by the
wall is Charloun Rieu. As Mistral wrote in the stanzas cancelled from *Mirèio*:

> "Ah! Calèndo, Calèndo, ounte èi ta douço pas?
> Ounte soun li caro risènto
> Dis enfantoun e di jouvènto?
> Ounte èi la man rufo e mouvènto
> Dòu vièi que fai la crous dessus lou sant repas!"

(Ah! Christmas, Christmas, where is your gentle peace?
Where are the laughing faces of the children and girls? Where
is the calloused but trembling hand of the old man blessing the
sacred meal?)

These two scenes from the past which he has reconstructed
with such loving care and detail commemorate two persons—
his mother and his father.

Thereafter we have a room devoted to the Castellane family,
then a wonderful collection of pottery, the music room (with
of course *galoubets* and *tambourins*) and a room dedicated
(since his death) to Mistral and the Félibres. We see his
cradle, and the blue velvet dress he was wearing as a small boy
when he fell in the ditch trying to pick yellow iris; and photographs of the Font-Ségugne group, and many interesting
books and photographs. Then—how right!—comes the gallery
of the Revolution (mostly official proclamations suppressing
something)—and that is that. I wish I had the talent to make
you see and enjoy it, but look for yourself.

"Separated from the continent by a long war, the English
at the end of the last century (eighteenth) had kept their
customs and their national character. There was still a
people. . . . That jealous class, the *bourgeoisie*, did not

197

exist. . . . Everything was not machinery in the manu-
facturing classes, folly in the privileged class. On the very
pavements where one now meets men in frock-coats or with
dirty faces, one used to see girls with straw hats tied under
their chins with a ribbon, who blushed if you even looked at
them." (Chateaubriand, *Mémoires d'Outre Tombe*, 1822.)

Chateaubriand wrote that of another country and before
Mistral was born, yet he too seems to have suspected that
'Progress' may cost more than it is worth, may even destroy the
real life of the people it is supposed to benefit.

In spite of the honours and money which came to him in his
later years Mistral made no change in the arrangements of his
way of life. More than once he was urged to stand as a candidate for the French Parliament, and of course in a local
constituency nobody would have had a chance against him.
He refused, as he refused the Académie and the Institut. As
he wrote Mariéton on one such occasion: "We have always
gone along with the poor. We must stay with them." (*Nous
avons fait route avec les pauvres. C'est avec eux qu'il faut rester.*) The
only portion of the Nobel half-prize which did not go to the
Museon was "given to a poor Félibre for whom Mistral had a
great respect." It might have been Tavan, but I like to think it
was poor Charloun Rieu, whose life had been so hard and
whose literary pension from the French Government (for
which Mistral had to work very hard) amounted to the handsome annuity of three hundred gold francs, about £32 of our
money. A worthy rival to the lavish generosity to poets of
Her Britannic Majesty's Government.

It is said that for about fifteen years Mistral gave up every
Thursday to work on his Museon in Arles. He never bought
himself a horse and trap to drive to the Graveson station, but
always took the local omnibus and then the train. When
people began to have motor-cars, somebody suggested that it
would be a great convenience for him to have one for his
weekly visit to Arles; but he wouldn't have it. "*Restons avec
les pauvres*". He did this so effectively that Ajalbert hints that

Mistral allowed the town of Arles to get more of the Swedish crowns than it ought to have had for the building. What does it matter? He created there something which seems a contradiction in terms—a Museum which is alive.

And now, with his work done, the time arrived for Mistral to think of his own departure and resting-place. There are stories that in his old age he went out and bought a crucifix, since it would not do for the author of *Mirèio* to die without having a crucifix in his bedroom. The "election of his sepulchre", as Ronsard phrased it, was highly characteristic. Near Les Baux is the small building known as Queen Joanna's Pavilion. She was murdered in 1382, and the Pavilion in question was in fact built in 1581 by order of Jeanne (or Joanna) de Quiqeran, Baroness of Les Baux. But the peasants confounded the two Joannas, and attributed the building to the "Reino Jano", which was enough for Mistral. His tomb in the churchyard at Maillane is a rather unhandy copy of Queen Joanna's Pavilion, which he had prepared beforehand. But, after all, surely a charming gesture? I am not quite so sure about the inscription:

"Non nobis, Domine, non nobis,
Sed nomini tuo
Et Provinciæ nostræ
Da gloriam."

It is a curious but authentic fact that the women of Maillane refused to put on their best clothes for President Poincaré* when he came to the village in 1913. Now, Mistral was angry about this, as he was outraged by the action of the Municipal Council in refusing to greet the President! Mistral was forced to send for the Official Register, in which he wrote:

"Acò's la signaturo dou Presidènt de la Republico Ramoun Poincaré, lou jour que venguè à Maiano vèire lou felibre Maianen, II d'òutobre 1913. F. Mistral."

* Poincaré had been denounced for not going to church.

He did well to be angry, for the whole nasty little episode was due to Charles Maurras and the silly propaganda of the *Action Française*. Mistral, in his candour and essential sweetness, always wanted the Félibrige to include everyone who loved or seemed to love Provence. But here Mistral's virtue and innocence were no defence. He should never have encouraged that political snake, who was all the more dangerous because he did know Provence. Mistral was not a Fascist, and Maurras made him seem to be one.

We come to the last scene of all. Many efforts had been made, Cardinal de Cabrières had intervened, the Pope had sent a benediction—received by Mistral and his wife on their knees —but he still hadn't gone to confession and taken the sacrament. The inference is obvious—he did not really believe, but he did not wish to shock the feelings of his neighbours. Human respect, I think they call it. Yet it was the Maillane church which killed him.

It was in March 1914—March, when the mistral is often its coldest and deadliest. The Maillane church was to have a new bell, for which Mistral had written a line or two to be engraved on it. At five o'clock in the evening of a bitterly cold March day the curé came fussing round about the inscription, and Mistral and his wife, just returned from their walk, were dragged off to approve it. As Mistral took off his hat at the entrance of the freezing cold church, he shuddered, and said: *"Eici far pas caud."* (It's not warm here.) When he managed to get away, he told his wife he had taken cold—it was bronchitis. On the 25th he suddenly became worse, and was obviously dying. His wife called to him to implore the Saintes Maries, and his last recorded words were *"Li Santo! Li Santo!"* By the time the curé reached him, it was too late, and he died without confession but with 'conditional absolution'. He lived eighty-three years and six months, and, as he had wished, was buried in the cemetery of Maillane under the reproduction of Queen Joanna's Pavilion. As far back as 1907 he wrote this poem on the tomb he had constructed:

"Near at hand I can see the close and the white cupola where like the snails I shall curl down for eternity.

"Last effort of our pride to escape devouring time—today or tomorrow it soon fades to a long oblivion.

"People will say to the peasants—Jan di Figo or Jan di Guèto: 'What's that dome?' And they'll answer: 'The Poet's tomb.

"'He was one who made songs for a pretty Provençal girl they called Mirèio; there are as many of them as there are gnats in the Camargue, "'Scattered about everywhere. . . . But he stayed in Maillane, and there are still old fellows about here who remember seeing him walking along the footpaths.'

"A later day will come, and they'll say: 'They made him king of Provence, but his name survives only in the call of the brown crickets.'

"And then, at their wits' end to explain, they'll say: 'He must have been a magician, the monument has on it the image of a star with seven rays.'"

Montpellier,
St. Roch's Day, 1955.

INDEX